Righting the Wrongs of the Enemy

MONDLI P. MALINGA
EMASWATI KINGDOM

Righting THE Wrongs OF THE ENEMY

MONDLI P. MALINGA
mondlipmalinga.co.za

Table of Contents

INTRODUCTION

*T*here are numerous speculations and narratives among different kinds of historians regarding our existence and where we all come from.

Some appear in a form of Izanusi *(the knowledge keepers), naturalists and philosophers (who mainly adopt their thoughts from the Divine).*

But, there are historians who are influenced by certain measures which are based on money rather than the book or information itself. I personally think that's where the conflict begins. That's because history is based on the past, and if there's anything that will remain unchanged and unshaken, it is the past for it carries much greater weight than what we're anticipating about what is said to be in the future— the unknown.

This then made certain events and significant figures in our history. Most of it originated in Africa, only for them to be stolen. Hence, it being never documented caused it to be vulnerable and became a "dance floor" for foreign but manipulative book writers. They took advantage of our true stories, true lives, true culture, traditions, true heritage and true events and figures to whom we paid our respects. They took advantage of our nature and being, therefore, our integrity which represents itself as uBuntu.

And then, Poof!

Our pride and dignity went south together with our stolen culture through stories which were told untruthfully and some even unfairly.

However, the impact of the manipulation and betrayal of Westerners upon Africans was mothered by the measurable scale of uBuntu *that our forefathers had for visitors. This led to our stories falling into hands of wrongdoers who then took advantage of documenting our stories before we learnt how to read and write.*

But that can only be devoured by African writers rewriting history. That's all.

So, yah!

That's what I'm about to do based on what I've been privileged to be. A philosopher, artist and a naturalist with a high voltage therefore, currency of "spirituality". My natural interconnectedness with nature is one which is orchestrated by the Universe itself. Nature being the provider of all, including information through the signals, numbers and words attained through dreams and visions of the philosopher that I am. This has never limited me from seeking more truth from many different platforms in the name of research to make this an interesting read.

And remember, this is to enjoy rather than to endure. So, please enjoy!

Southwards From The North

In the beginning, there was the aba-Ngoni (those who do not sin). They are the oldest race on Earth to be precise. Their name is derived from the Ngoni word *uKona* which means "to sin".

However, our forefathers relied more on wisdom than education, which is the mother of education after all.

Hence, their approach towards naming their race abaNgoni opposed to present-day amaNguni, which lacks proper meaning.

Lol! Imagine being a sinner coming from a different world filled with sinners, including yourself and you get to meet an entire race calling themselves abaNgoni. Then, when you try and investigate deeper as to what in the seven hells that means, you are told it means "those who do not sin". Lol! Wouldn't you want to do anything in your power to want to change the meaning of this name, especially if the owners of the name have not yet documented and preserved it in writing somewhere or somehow?

Of course, this is obvious: The name was likely to have been tampered with by those who already knew how to read and write or possessed a skill of manipulation in their hands, full of multiple ways of sinning.

Then, in 1823, the AbaNgoni or Ngoni language was transformed into isiZulu in honour of King Shaka Zulu by the British missionary, Henry Callaway. You may recall that it is believed that the legendary Zulu king ruled from 1816 to 1828. Therefore, it makes perfect sense that the introduction of isiZulu was to honour him.

However, the grammar and orthography (spelling system) come from the Ngoni language. This is why many isiZulu words sound similar to the language of the ancient abaNgoni people. They have the same ethnic characteristics, but certain words, including the name of their race *(AbaNgoni)* was a big threat to the British Empire. Hence, it had to be changed to shift it out of its original meaning and context.

That is why we have the terms AbaNguni or Nguni people. However, if you are asked to translate the meaning of these words, you'd be lost for words because it is just a meaningless word. It was created to bring meaning, but instead, it did the opposite, which is nonsense.

It is for this reason that the generations who came later never understood the meaning of their name, which in its own sense possessed a good representation of what they were supposed not to do, and that was to never sin.

So, now that we have been reminded of who we truly are, with or without religion, we need to be then reminded of where we come from. The Ngoni race dates back to before the Golden Age of Egypt, a civilisation that astonished our forefathers. We were already non-sinners by then, which then means we never needed to be told by any form of religion not to sin. Our forefathers had already made it mandatory that we should be non-sinners and even named an entire race, AbaNgoni.

I'm not sure if you understand this.

So, where do Ngoni people come from?

Well, I think this becomes a purposeful question because we come from the north, a place that is now known as Cameroon. This was the land of the Ngoni people, but this was only after the Exodus.

I am referring to the biblical account of the Israelites' escape from slavery. The exact date has sparked debate over the centuries, with some experts saying that we don't need to know the truth about what happened and when.

Exodus was the genesis of our problems because as some fled from Ramses II and headed to the west and east, some lingered around Africa in desperation and sought help from clans in the region. These clans expanded over time and led to the formation of the Ngonu race. The languages of those who sought help differed and a new language was formed with influence from older languages such as Hebrew and Hindi.

Hebrew was a language that was spoken openly by slaves in ancient Egypt. It mothered many different languages which were shared amongst what was then a fast-growing community of newer nations.

Those who fled from Egypt were angry after being enslaved for many years.

They found it awkward to live normal lives as the AbaNgoni were accustomed to. They came from Egypt with many traditions which were new and not in alignment with what the AbaNgoni believed in.

Some of our forefathers decided to leave Kwa-Bantu, the AbaNgoni land which is today known as Cameroon. Soon, they were scattered across Africa. They were already mixed with Hebrew-speaking nations and this created an auto-division and resulted in what we call today races and tribes (I will unpack a few of these).

For now, I want us to look into what this auto-division manufactured rather than only understanding the difference between a race and a tribe. This will also allow us to understand culture and traditions, allowing us to see the full picture.

It is only when we are on the same page that we can properly understand the difference between a race and a tribe.

Answering these two questions will assist us in finding our paths to mental freedom and not being confused as to who and what we are.

Well, in the simplest of terms: A tribe is a group of people whose beliefs or faiths are based on a shared cultural and social identity such as language, traditions and history, despite physical differences. Often, a tribe has a common ancestor or origin story but tribes can change over time.

On the other hand, a race is a group whose faiths are based on physical characteristics classification such as skin colour, facial features and hair texture.

So, this must then give us understanding of who the emaSwati are and will also allow us to go a little deeper into why they remained emaSwati. These were actually families who shared the same history, ancestry and traditions and then later shared a single goal of

migrations towards the southern region of the continent, from the Great Lakes region in Central Africa.

They travelled from one place to the next, heading
southwards as they traced the River Nile. They travelled with their livestock, hence they needed to be
near water. They travelled until they found their first
home in what is known today as Tanzania where
another group of abaNgoni are still living to this day.

However, over time while they were enjoying their long
stay in Tanzania, they were tracked by other groups
causing their 'cultural pollution' to grow and expand
as they too multiplied. They then continued expanding
southwards in search of more land and resources.

However, these weren't the only reasons why they
migrated. As I mentioned, it was a combination of
factors, including that they were and still are a very
independent "national character". They started trading
with others before they reached Swaziland. Did you
know that amongst all the abaNgoni people, the
emaSwati were the first to search for access to trade
and commerce? They formed many trade routes and
exchanged goods along the coast of the Indian Ocean.
Oh! I can see you did not know that. They traded with
foreign buyers and sellers, exchanging goods such as
iron and salt. Now, isn't that something?

They were a group of very wise individuals who had a
clear vision of what they wanted. Remember, this was
a tribe and amongst them were a mixture of thinkers,
including the Hebrews, who may have already

adapted to speaking the isiNgoni language and thus the isiSwati language. Some knew how to count, read, write and farm, given their previous lives as slaves when they lived in Egypt. More than a million slaves escaped from Egypt and so, they were concerned about having to be in other conflicts, which could lead to wars.

As they were then associated with certain groups of the newer races from Egypt, they didn't want anything to stop them from finding fertile ground to continue farming and raising cattle. The emaSwati tribe was also respected for being skilled cattle herders who were searching for fertile land in which they could settle down permanently and raise their livestock and also raise their children.

This was difficult to do as they carried a heavy weight on their shoulders. Soon, their cultural and traditional structures resonated with many abaNgoni clans and many of the former slaves who fled the Egyptian leadership of Pharaoh Thutmose whose warriors were believed to be after them.

In a way, they had lost their identity and needed something new to adhere to.

It was during this era that many words, names and their meanings were easily confused by the newer generations in the world which was in "Black & White Picture".

It was during this era when our ancestors were believed to be gods and alien beings, and we were their offspring. But, who introduced the concept of God?

For the name God could be given to one who was superior in nature and in features or who possessed unique supernatural powers. This is just like our forefathers who possessed magnitudes of telepathy in their doings, and their spiritual vibrations were felt across the earth. They possessed a built-in survival skill. It was our forefathers who discovered the understanding of extracting and making iron from rocks to making tools and weapons.

Over the years, they developed a remarkable built-in strategy for warfare. The skill of building houses was first discovered by our forefathers who also introduced the art and culture of teaching and learning. They had already put in place a set of rules to live by (which were against anything evil) including that it was forbidden to eat meat. This was after the Exodus when owning cattle became popular, however, it was mainly for offerings or sacrificial purposes.

It was said to have been brutal and rigid and some would consider it *Ingozi* (danger), a word which was later transformed out of its own but had an important meaning as it was later (when Ngoni language was changed into Zulu language which was then documented). This word read as *Idlozi.*

This means that it was never in our culture to own any livestock let alone slaughter anything that moves, including cows, sheep and goats, especially to feast. You will recall that added to our number was a group of newer races and tribes from Egypt and some of them used to worship these animals as gods back in Egypt.

These were the "links" that added to the growth of emaSwati's population and then later added to traditions. Therefore, auto-division occurred caused by the pressure of change.

The more the population grew, the more tradition started influencing the community of those who were believed to be abaNgoni (those who do not sin). The culture was common in both what was developing to be newer races and newer tribes and that of ancient abaNgoni (our ancestors). Traditions forced them to differ from one family to the next but they were in the same spectrum of being either tribes or races that they were expanding to become. You will remember that unlike races, tribes are highly likely to change over time. This is because they're not based on physical classification but similarities found in the midst of their individual differences as a group of individuals with the same goal.

In short, the art of raising livestock came from the likes of the Hindu people who originated from the first community of slaves, formed by the Hebrew people of Egypt. Amongst them were ancient Chinese (whose skins were brown and some even darker). Their resemblances and features originated from the tribe of Basuthu people. However; their "seed" was widespread across many different nations. Some of these were new at the time, including the AmaZulu clan and so forth.

This made the abaNgoni group to be slightly unique in their own sense and manner of doing different things. They possessed a greater amount of *ubuntu* gestures as culture and this always made people want to be part of their consistent movement and goals. They were respected for maintaining unity despite what was becoming newer traditions that different families would choose to adapt and adhere to.

Their rapid expansion and growth in knowledge and wisdom ensured that they easily divided or defeated in any manner. You either joined them or left them. Not only were they humble, calm and respectable, they were the most feared tribe in history and also known for being the most dangerous tribe on Earth, They were feared by the likes of the pharaohs of Ancient Egypt.

They were never colonised by the Egyptians whose forces were defeated many times by ancient abaNgoni people as they tried to invade what was then Kwa-Bantu (modern day Cameroon). Even though they had their differences in traditions, they still embraced one culture of unity and *ubuntu* (humanity).

They also had one strategy in warfare and this was that they were united as Ngoni-speaking groups.

This made them a strong group, who fought against anyone who was not aligned with their culture.

I am using the name emaSwati to try and accommodate everyone and keep you in the light of understanding about who I am talking about.

The name emaSwati is new but they were once known as the Adza or the Hadzabe people, the oldest and most dangerous tribe in the world.

The Hadzabe Or Hadza Tribe

Along their long travels, a lot was changing over time. This includes their language which was influenced by a fusion of multiple languages which later formed Swahili or Kiswahili.

This was the Hazdas (who later became known as emaSwati). They had to develop along the way in order to help meet each other's differences halfway. Hence, they were a combination of multiple ethnic groups whose languages were barriers for them to communicate and easily understand each other. So, they created Kiswahili, a language that combined every language that was spoken by all the different groups from the north who had to travel longer distances from the north heading southwards. Another reason that made them create a new language is that they were trying to avoid wars.

It was believed that the pharaohs would send their troops to come to look and drag their slaves back to Egypt. By then, some of them had already become fathers, mothers and grandparents to some members of what was then slowly developing to be emaSwati whose Ngoni language was becoming lighter and lighter by time during their long stay in Tanzania. As a result, the Kiswahili languages' grammar was sharpened.

As I mentioned, it was not only about creating a new language but it was also much easier to disguise themselves from their enemies.

As they travelled towards Tanzania, they had a single goal but it changed when they reached that country. This was due to auto-division caused by changes in traditions and other factors such as food security and expansion. This also added to the factors that triggered racial bridges getting much wider and making sizable gaps between those groups.

There was the Ngoni people (who still spoke Ngoni) and the Hadzas (who spoke Swahili). The Hazdas were a smaller group under the umbrella of the Ngoni group but were expanding with time.

But, that's when the Ngoni group discovered that they always gained strength from the Hadzas or the Hadzabe people. They would stop at nothing to defeat the enemy.

This was followed by the Hadzas' defeat of the Ngoni race in a fight for settlement in Tanzania. After that battle, the population of the Hadzabe people gained momentum. Remember, it was the "numbers game" because the more the population of each group grew, the better it was for them.

This worked to their advantage in many ways. They needed warriors and wise men in their leadership structures such as pathfinders, soothsayers, healers, etc. Hence, expansion was vital. However, it was this battle that caused division among the AbaNgoni groups. Soon, racism grew among these groups, resulting in breakaways that formed many different empires. This included AmaXhosa, AmaNdebele, AmaZulu, AbaSotho and emaSwati.

I like the story behind the Hadza *or* Hadzabe people. Later, they became known as the Hadzebes or Bo-Hadzebe or Radebe or Hadebe. To me, this shares a huge link to who and what the Hadza tribe was and what is said about them being the oldest tribe on Earth while the Nguni is the oldest race on Earth. It goes without saying that they dominated the Ngoni-speaking people and even reached the AbaSotho-speaking group.

Language Versus Time

In the early 11th century some of them first stepped foot on South African ground. They had migrated from Tanzania (where they lived for more than two centuries). Some went to other parts of the continent such as Kenya, Mozambique, Zambia, Namibia and Malawi.

However, the first Nguni land, Kwa-Bantu, originated from modern-day Cameroon.

Following social disputes and war, many of them migrated and some found "the land of milk and honey", as our former president, Thabo Mbeki, would say when referring to South Africa.

And this was where the Kiswahili language started to slowly fade away. This was between 1,500 and 1,800 years ago. While our forefathers found better and peaceful lands to settle on, they were also trying to preserve their origins, heritage and culture. They knew that these could be easily lost if they lost their own language.

People, language is very important, especially your own mother tongue.

Hence, some are still lost to this day, thinking that *Amasiko* means culture. This is a good example of the negative impact that has been caused by the transformation in languages.

This is especially due to the time factor which has polluted our languages and left us with words of which there's no known meaning or understanding of. That is why we lack answers to many questions to this day.

Well, the word *Amasiko* is a word derived from *Sika* or *Ukusika* in Ngoni. In English, it means "to cut". It stems from an era when certain groups engaged themselves in certain cults and followed a set of traditions that included *Usiko* (the process of skin cutting). This was also known as *Ukuklekla* as opposed to *Ukugqaba,* which both involve an almost similar process that entails the skin being cut using *unkhonto* (spear) or knives.

This tradition fascinated some families and they used it to hide their identity from their enemies. The act became popular amongst the Ngoni-speaking people across the southern regions of African. However, this tradition may have originated in the north and was brought to the south when people migrated to that region.

The name for these tribes or groups would differ from one place to the next and from one tribe to the other.

They were known to be *izichaza* which also was polluted by time and later sounded like *iziqhaza* with an "Q" as opposed to a "C". Such differences were founded within the abaNgoni-speaking group, derived from a Ngoni word referring to an act of "explaining" (*ukuChaza*).

But, before we're reminded of what they looked like, why do you think they were called *izichaza* meaning explainers?

Well, we all know it is traditions that differentiate one group from another. Some families didn't find it necessary to engage in those practices and became the talk of the village.

This was because they were part of a cult that they may have joined during their migration to different parts of Africa which forced them to get "marked". However, some found it unnecessary to hide their identity or to do so for other reasons, let alone join anything they didn't understand and end up being cut. This includes cutting their faces and other parts of their bodies, including their private parts and ears. The *Izichaza* or *Iziqhaza* would be identified by their cut ears. They would then have to explain to other clans why they had cut their ears.

Basically, they would cut through the bottom part of their ears and insert a piece of wood to create a sizable hole. This is much different compared to the size of a modern-day earring.

The holes in the *Izichaza's* ears were so big that one could easily put their arms through them. They would have a circle or ring of some sort on the bottom part of their ears. This would then leave the skin on the bottom part of their ears hanging causing an imperfect diameter of about 30 to 60mm in between the top and the hanging bottom part of each of their ear. And for some reason, if not pain, they were a very grumpy and violent group of individuals amongst the abaNgoni clans. Some would call them *Izinzule*. This is another word which lost its meaning with time because the actual formation of the word comes from their actions of going from one place to the next. This was called *ukuzula*, hence their name was derived from a word known as *zula* (going from one place to the next).

This then means that their name, *izinzule*, was mistaken for *iziNzuli* (the travellers). These groups were isolated from many other abaNguni clans and were not accepted into these groups.

That's because many of these people were believed to have been practicing and performing different traditions within their cults and hence, they had to move from one place to the next.

Another thing that we need to know is that *Amasiko* (the processes of skin cutting) caused division amongst abaNgoni-speaking clans. This later resulted in the formation of the amaXhosa, abeSothu and amaNdebele clans.

It was indeed a questionable style which was also quite new at the time. However, like I mentioned, many other "skin cutters" emerged as time went by. Not all of those cuts were similar. Some would cut through their ears but others cut off part of their private parts. Today, this is known as initiation or *Ukuwela* or *Ukweluka* in Xhosa and *Ukusoka* or *Ingoma* in Zulu-speaking groups. Added to that is Kwa-Nongoma, a place where some Zulus were engaged in *Ingoma* or *Ukusoka*. This stems from a Ngoni word, *i-Soka* (a player). Hence, it was believed that those boys who've been to *Ingoma* and got their penis skin cut were loved by girls. But, to some, it was just another form of trying to hide their identity and to a transform into newer tribes which they did.

Some would cut their faces, preferably on their foreheads and cheeks. Others would cut their backs and chests in the name of *uKuklekla* (not *Ukugqaba* or *Ukugcaba*).

The act went as far as some clans having to cut off certain parts of their bodies in a practice that was similar to initiation. Some people would cut off their fingers or toes to be accepted as part of those tribes.

This has been confused as being part of the culture of AbaNgoni people but, in actual fact, this was only a tradition practiced by four in ten families.

However, because the Ngoni-speaking people dominated the southern parts of Africa (despite the fact that they were then mixed with the newer races and tribes from Egypt, Mali and Ethiopia etc. due to wars, who many of which were believed to be slightly different in terms of belief systems), it was then believed that the majority of the Ngoni people were involved in that cult. It was believe that its members had to cut their skin to belong to the cult. So, you'd understand because *vele,* many people of the time didn't understand these newer but weird ways in which many people were engaging.

These were just like many other changes that came about at the time. For example, when coloured people chose to remove their teeth, this cannot be attributed to *uSiko* because they didn't actually cut anything but they performed their own tradition like many that we have.

It was these kinds of happenings that made many other groups who were part of the AbaNgoni race adapt to what the newer races and tribes were doing, especially when they claimed to have done so to protect themselves. Hence, even those ceremonies were conducted by traditional healers or carefully selected elders of the group.

It was even believed that those who cut themselves possess a unique power. This was associated with *Izinyamazane* (a mixture of herbs and certain animal parts). This is different to *muthi* (which are simply dried plants or herbs).

Remember, this was an era when the ships had not yet landed with "the western kind of religion" which was designed in Africa and mastered in Greece and Rome. By mastered, I mean being edited in the name of manipulation. It is no longer a secret that religion is used as some kind of a weapon by a few but to help destroy the majority.

So, that's where and how the auto-division kicked in because people differed from each other as a result of their traditions. Some believed in the power of plants or herbs. They were not in alignment with the processes of *Amasiko,* which is the mother to what was known as *Ukuklekla* (skin cutting). By the way, the word *muthi* or *imithi* was an ancient AbaNgoni word that referred to plants in general, including grasses, flowers and trees. But later, more components (dried animal parts) were added to *muthi* or herbs to actually turn *uMuthi* to what was later known to be *Izinyamazane* (the animals) or *Ingoma.* This may be confusing because *Ingoma* is known to be a song. This is true but not in the context of traditional healing and killing. That's because the original word meant something else before it meant song. As such, there is a need to explain it origin and how it came to mean what it does today.

Ingoma can actually mean the kind of herbs which are mixed with certain animal parts which would normally be used in spells. Some of these spells are recited in the form of a song, hence the word *idngoma.*

Even though the tone may have been verbalised, it still means 'song' and that's why *Izangoma* (musicians) were needed. They were required to sing while certain spells were commanded to the *muthi* or *ingoma*being utilised in that particular space or ritual.

This means that this group of people have been given the power that don't even deserve. *Izangoma* were actually the processes or practices that *Iziyanga* wouldn't have done or achieved the best results. Should the word not mean 'spell' or 'song' instead?

Soon, these practices became more popular and they became known as the *Izinyanga* people as opposed to *Izinyanga* beings (the creatures of our moon).

So, before we move any further there's nothing like *Isiko* or *usiko* being our "culture". No, that is just nonsense. Because even to this date, skin cutting is never for every Ngoni group or should I say for everyone in our heritage. I have to wrap this one up nicely this way because we'll keep on embracing a word of something that doesn't even exist. Our actual culture is *uBuntu* (humanity) as it exists across all nations as long as they are black. Another similarity that could be confusing but interesting is the concept of what culture is explained to be in the manner in which we dance as African people. It is said that Africa is a continent of calm, wise and humble people whose instincts seem to be on point and similar to their very own choices that built their characteristics as Africans.

But why do I say this?

You'd recall that Africans possess a built-in connection with nature and the divine and the sciences of life itself. Survival and happiness run through our veins. A better example would be the way we dance. This proves that the science of life runs in our veins and is part of our instincts.

As you'd recall, we'd normally do with anything to do with the "ground" being chanted on over and over again when we dance as this alone is deeper than just dancing. It has a deeper meaning because it entails an act of causing a significant scientific phenomenon known as friction which is formed by our feet grinding and bumping against the ground as we stomp, slide and jump on it. This produces an energy called kinetic energy which, when you dance, is transformed into many but vital energies that you may need at the time or even after the dance.

This means that through dancing we get to recharge. This then gives us a level of connectivity with the earth, nature and the universal signals. Therefore, the Universe itself as the energy would be bouncing back and forth between you and the earth. Hence, dancing is classified with many but other spiritual mediums of connection with the Universe. That's why when a dancer dances and mind you, I'm talking of what I know for sure because I too used to dance a lot when I was younger. Trust me, there more I danced; I'd feel something inside me or perhaps outside me but capable of making me do the dance moves. It was like some type of electricity or unexplainable energy. It was a weird kind of warm energy. It was this and then that, then a cold sweat dripping down my spine, increasing the electrical current in my doings and the way that I would think during a dance.

The thoughts of moving according to the beat and the thoughts of changing my moves happened rapidly and naturally. At times, I'd find myself doing what was never on my 'menu' and believe me, I think every dancer would tell you the same thing. That something weird would normally happen only when you're dancing. It is like a vibrational force takes over as the kinetic energy reduces. Then, the heat, electricity, beat and the cold sweat would keep me moving like a robot and people couldn't help but watch me dance. It's not easy to explain this but I guess the least of what I shared would help give you some clarity as you picture the moment, especially because it's coming directly from the horse's mouth. There really is some kind of energy that we create by dancing.

And that's one similarity that African people possess within and amongst themselves. It is an instinct that can provoke certain elements of what I call the universal signals, which work as a spiritual connection between man and the Divine or the Higher Power when 'melted' down upon us. The energies that we normally provoke by our dances are not all cut from the same cloth. By that, I mean just that. Further, they're not cooked in the same pot by the same chef.

In short, some dances have different meanings from other dances. They vary in genre and occasion when they are danced. Perhaps, I should explain briefly what I mean by this.

You will recall that Africans are simple people. We love to be happy. Full stop. And that is obvious to see, isn't it?

But we're not on Earth alone, are we? This then wrestles with what African people in general are about, which is fun or simply having a good time.

But then, there are some out there who make it their duty to wake up every morning to find ways of disturbing our happiness, to win our peace in exchange for lonely, toxic lives. And sure, we're living them unapologetically, aren't we?

So, because of the change in time, a lot of the under-standing of life's pieces also changed. Hence, there were and still are dances. Therefore, the energies which were aimed for before and after wars and battles. Some dances were only used in celebra-tions and various ceremonies. There are dances and songs for celebrating ceremonies such as *Umemulo* (wedding). These would be different to those performed at a *Lobola* ceremony. During *Umemulo* the expected dances would be *Ukushikila*, performed by young virgin ladies and girls (*Amatshithsi*) and *ukukikizela* (ululation) or *uKulilizela* performed by the mamas, aunties and grannies of the village where the ceremony of *Umemulo* was held. Also, the young men (*Amabhungu*) would perform *Ukusina*.

On the other hand, during a *Lobola* ceremony, the dances and songs would comprise what emaSwati people would call *Ukucobosha*. It is expected that both the bride's and groom's families would perform a series of competitive gestures all in the name of fun and celebrating the occasion.

This performance would usually have a shared theme and dance routines where the families would actu-ally be supported by the young boys and girls who form the young blood membership of that family's given communities.

Both of these would never be similar to the dance a grandfather would briefly perform when his lost cow is brought back home. This is a dance known as *Ukugiya* (which is often done when someone is celebrating a certain jubilant moment or as an intro or perhaps even an outro for a certain occasion).

But then, there's a dance that ancient warriors would normally perform prior and after battles or wars. This was called *Indlamu* (from a short phrase used for hit en in ancient isiNgoni language). It is a noun that refers to *Indla-Mu-ntu,* a serious killer as opposed to *Ukugida* (for moments of honour or praise). This could be in the form of a dance or a song. Hence, there were a group of elders who would be known or believed to be performers of *Isiqhathamiya* (derived from *Ukuqathama,* a Nguni word for moving very slowly). This was also known as <u>*Ukugida*</u> *Ingoma Busuku* where, during ancient times, a few elders were in a secret cult whose members only met at night. It was believed that they used to praise (hence *ukuGida*) sacred spirits found in the mountains (*Ekuphakameni*).

However, time has mixed it all up and today every dance performance that has a chant in it is mistakenly called *Ukugida.* However, that is not the case here. Well, both *Ukugida* and *ukushaya Indlamu* dances appear almost similar to one another. However, I have mentioned that *Indlamu* would often not have a good ending. As I said, it would normally be performed by warriors (*iButho*) prior and after battle just like gladiators do. Maybe you should watch the build-up of a rugby game to see what I mean. It was a way to awaken the *iButho's* spirits by provoking them through songs (spells) and dances.

The *Indlamu* dance, like many other traditional dances, would actually comprise acts of certain, but strong and feared animals. You could only identify these by the way the *iButho* or their representatives shaped their arms in the air as they prepared to beat their feet against the ground as though they were on a battlefield. This would often represent the horns of an animal such as a buffalo or a bull.

For example, these dancers would often lift their hands in the air and form a horn-like structure above their heads. They would also dig their feet but before doing so, they slide and scratch their feet on the ground in a backwards motion. This is similar to an angry bull who is ready to charge.

Furthermore, the mamas and gogos would mimic the actions of a chicken during *ukukikizela* (ululation) or *uKulilizela* — which is a sound attached to an act that they'd make as they scream at the top of their voices. This is similar to what chickens do and sound like when they see something interesting or strange or any sort of change in the environment they're in. So, it was not only *iButho* or *aMabutho* (plural form) that would perform these acts of powerful and feared animals to either intimidate their enemy or to express their feelings of honour or celebration.

This could actually be something we can hold on to as part of the culture of African people and not *Amasiko* which are partly scattered amongst the African nations' heritages. This is also the case amongst the abaNgoni groups to whom many of which never adhered to the processes of *Amasiko.*

But, I'm glad we're having these kinds of discussions today. But for now we're about to explore "me and you".

And besides, it was this *usiko* conversation which led us here. So, by wrapping it nicely, it is a good way of questioning it.

Now that we all know what *muthi, Izinyamazane* and *Ingoma* meant in ancient times, I think it would be good to know what the word *Nyamazane* meant in the *muthi* context and what it meant to our forefathers.

Inyamazane was an ancient Ngoni word referring to any kind of animal. Remember, this wasn't in the Zulu or isiZulu language but rather in the AbaNgoni language to which isiZulu had to be its own supplement.

The Ngoni language is more than a million years old compared to isiZulu which dates back to 1823. There was a huge threat attached to the existence of the AbaNgoni language.

It was a rich language and in fact, the English language didn't even exist when the Ngoni language was already mushrooming across the African continent. Even the *lingua franca* of the people of the skies of Zeus spoke French. This then means that the majority of their offspring communicated in French because even English is made up of many languages, including French.

Well, that's not where we are. Perhaps, you should read *The Book of Mondli* to get more information on this subject. Right now, I would like us to explore even deeper and look into who or what *Izinyanga* were.

That's because, it is the truth that shall set all of us free. Free from captivity and free from not knowing what is going on to what has always been going on without many people knowing what life has become and what they have become.

A lot got lost with time. Languages changed and this then changed the manner in which life was viewed by the people, both past and present. As a result, a lot of the truth has been hidden from us.

So, who were the Nyanga people?

Look, the aim is not to cause discrimination but to open a portal for the Malinga family and extended parties linked to it via 'bio links' to know the truth. That's all. Yah! That's about it.

Well, *Izinyanga* were people from the moon. Oops! Another can of worms is opening up...

This is like many other races, newer races that originate from many different worlds and planets. This included the nine as opposed to millions of planets we were made or programmed not to know about.

The creatures of the moon were helpful to the enhancement of understanding just beyond living as man. They opened our forefathers to complement what was then a new understanding of life on Earth and how the systems of the Universe worked.

This included sacrifice for the creatures of outer Earth and will forever be 'the something for something' beings.

Let us go back to life in Egypt which was where civilisation on Earth has its starting point. We will also look at the influence of creatures from outer Earth, including those from the moon.

In the early stages of the development in Egypt, it was believed that civilisation began there and spread throughout the planet. Why?

Back then, Earth was one solid piece of ground; there were no divisions. The centre of Earth was where Egypt stands even today. This means that this operation was indeed planned and led by creatures from above who were able to determine the centre of the earth.

They needed proper ways to measure distance and determine the centre of the earth which, at the time, was far beyond man's thinking.

This is especially true because back then the earth was still young and there was no technology. This then proves that the Egyptian Empire was not only built by man but supernatural interventions were involved. To this day, no engineer or scientist can do what those creatures did thousands of years ago despite all the technology we have in the 21st century. Think about that.

Some of those creatures were called the Black Headed Kings. Later, when other creatures from other planets started invading while some migrated to our planet to seek citizenship from the Black Headed Kings, a lot started going wrong. For they gave citizenship to the wrong creatures whose idea was to later take over the planet from them. Some of these creatures are believed to have originated from the moon.

Egypt, during this time; was actually the world's airport (if I may put it that way) and it was where UFOs and spaceships used to land or were supposed to land. Egypt played a huge part in having Earth controlled and monitored by alien alliances. That's because it was the greatest empire at the time.

But, like I mentioned, the problems of Earth began when more and more creatures from outer Earth started dominating and spreading throughout the planet.

This included the Titans (the group to which Kronos, the father of Zeus, belonged). They originated from the Planet Uranus and were led by the Goddess Gaia. She who owned a gigantic spaceship and had an army of giant warriors. It was also believed she came from a very wealthy family. This was the group who later mothered the Greeks and Romans.

There was also the Anunnakid group who originated from the Planet Niburu. I'm sorry you had to find out this way but yes, there is a planet called Niburu. Their leader, Enlin, who preferred to be called God claims Earth as his.

He is father to the entire Indian race and the leader of a group who called themselves Samaritans (*Abasamariya abalungileyo*).

Please stick with this.

And then; there was a group from Planet Jupiter, led by the father of eagles whose name was Jupiter or Jove. His group actually belonged to one of the 12 famous moons of planet Jupiter, one which is called Europa.

Adding to the picture were the likes of Satan who originated on Planet Saturn. He was a scientific artist and only he possessed the potion from Andromeda to "put to sleep" the immortal leaders of different worlds. He could freeze them and make them seem dead but they were not. They were just frozen.

He was trusted and respected by many creatures of the skies. He goes by different names in many different worlds. Already, we know a couple, don't we? This includes Lucifer, the devil, Drago or the Dragon, Abaddon and Apollyon. Lol! I'm sorry for laughing but I like English people for being an open book to read sometimes. Here's a nice one, from the English version of the knowledge of who Satan is where he becomes "The Prince".

How did he become a prince?

The Bible talks about "one king" so how does he become a prince?

Well, I understand the translations or names of Satan of the likes of the Latin, Hebrew and Greek languages of the offspring of creatures from outer Earth; describing a singular figure. Then you know who we're dealing with here. Indeed, a deceiver!

Oh! Before I forget, here are two verses I'm referring to where Satan (the deceiver) is referred to as a prince.

John 12:31: "Now is the time for the judgement on this world, now the prince of this world will be driven out..."

John 14:30: "I will not say much more to you, for the prince of this world is coming. He has no hold on me."

Moving right on.

Together, the Titans, the Anunnaki, the 'Jews' from Jupiter and Satan (the prince of this world) as their frontier worked for six millennia and three centuries, 12,300 Earth years, nonstop. They tried to hack Earth and control its life forms.

However, magnitudes of anger, jealousy and envy resulted in pressure that was orchestrated by the fast-growing Egyptian civilisation which included man. At the time, Earth may have been known as Egypt. It included the valued leadership of eight planets and the Black Headed Kings who determined the rules. However, man was becoming a huge threat.

This then will retrace us to *Izinyanga* (the creatures from the moon). The word itself is derived from the ancient AbaNgoni's way of respect when referrring to the moon. Like Jupiter, Satan and many others, the creatures of our moon were also called by the name of the place of their origin. In this case, it was *Inyanga* or *Izinyanga* (referring to the moon).

These creatures were not easy to defeat as they possessed natural magic-like stunts including being invisible. They also travelled as part of the Black Headed Kings' crew who were believed to have originated from the moon too.

Their work was to help navigate the skies and to tell what was about to happen. They possessed an ability to see the past and foresee the future. Their language was brain language, meaning you wouldn't bother hiding your thoughts from them by saying what you didn't mean because they could detect and capture data from your brain while thinking. They hear your thoughts which makes words unnecessary. It wasn't what came from their mouths that counted but their brains.

This helped them communicate in every verbalised language on Earth and those of other humanoids from other worlds. They could get information about something by simply looking at or touching it. The only disadvantage was that they couldn't detect automated brains, such as those of Androids (android being a robot that looks exactly like a human). They were a version of humanoids from Andromeda, the darker and colder space millions of light years away from the sun.

The creatures of our moon resonated with our forefathers because they shared values and characteristics in their doings. Hence, our "being" and "nature" by aliens or creatures from outer Earth is known and strongly believed to suit those considered to be righteous. These beings (aliens) believe that he who can face the sunlight is considered righteous.

And it makes a lot of sense because demons are allergic to sunlight. And there we were, living our daily lives under the exposure of the sunlight. Hence, they had to make man of their own "mankind" out of our genes, magically and scientifically so.

Okay, speaking of mankind; the word itself tell us that these weren't really man but, "man types" or "man-like". The Adam and Eve type.

But those were not the only things that made those creatures resonate with our forefathers. They also fed on plants, fungus and roots and drank water. This was unlike many other creatures who kept on invading Earth from outer Earth. Instead, *Izinganga* had a very close relationship with nature. They believed everything organic. They lived in the mountains in caves and they preferred it that way.

Some were four-legged but they would, from time to time, use their front legs as their hands when necessary. However, amongst them was a different group with two legs and one eye.

They were very short human-like creatures around one metre tall. This was unlike the Black Headed Kings who were very tall. And amongst them were a different group of giants who were more organic as opposed to being extra-terrestrial and evil like their equals were. Their interests were based on more than just wielding power. They were looking for minerals.

Remember, this happened during what was known as "The Golden Age". Hence, Egypt then was indeed covered in gold. The entire city shone from a couple of thousands of Earth years away. This attracted a lot of attention from those who later became their enemy — whose offspring have grown to be our enemy too.

They were known and still are known for their love of what shines and reflects, that being nothing but mineral deposits.

I am referring to the Anunnaki group whose mission was focused on finding minerals. They possessed a unique power to control the masses' minds. This allowed them to drag them into slavery and dig for minerals. To date, this power is still used by secret organisations such as the Illuminati, Freemasons, Christianity and your famous 666s of this planet. There are numerous other organisations who exist to do evil.

They use a power called Masonic Mind Control to control our minds. This can be achieved by wearing a bracelet or a necklace. You know, just to keep things under cover and all. And those were actual gladiators and warriors who enslaved people with whips in their hands and sods on their waists but still called themselves "The Good Samaritan".

To me, they were nothing but founders of certain religious structures and cults because they were bloodthirsty deities.

So, about *Izinyanga* who were vegetarians and not blood thirsty. Their intention was to cause harm to no one except those who stood in the way of righteousness. They were the protectors of the structure of the kings of Egypt.

Even Amen Ra, the ruler of Egypt, adopted power and wisdom from them. These were the kinds of creatures who never needed flying saucers to get to the moon but magic. Their abilities did not originate on Planet Earth. So, these were the Nyanga beings of that time. But they were affected, especially after the Alexandra War which swept away a number of empires, including Egypt.

The war was over their shoulders and planned against the Egyptians for thousands of years led by a giant named Alexandra The Great and the 12 disguised and secret Gods of Christianity which are worshiped by both Greeks and Romans (the presenters of Christianity). These include (please pay close attention):

12 Greek gods, the Titans, originating from Planet Uranus

1. Zeus (known to have been the king of the gods, sky and thunder). It was the name Zeus which was later used to form the name Jesus. We will discuss further the shenanigans attached to the subject of Jesus.

2.   Poseidon (god of the sea and earthquakes)

3.   Hades (god of the underworld and the dead)

4.   Demeter (goddess of agriculture and fertility)

5.   Athena (goddess of wisdom, war and craft)

6.   Hera (queen of the gods, marriage and family)

7.   Apollo (god of the sun, music, poetry and prophecy) and a twin brother to Artemis.

8.   Artemis (goddess of hunting, wilderness and childbirth)

9.   Ares (god of war and violence). Are you kidding me?

10.   Aphrodite (goddess of love, beauty and desire)

11.   Hephaestus (god of fire, blacksmiths and volcanoes)

12.   Hermes (messenger god, commerce and travellers)

Like I advised, I sure hope you paid close attention to the above structure of the gods of Greece. It was led by Zeus; the son of two siblings (a sister and a brother); Kronos or Cronus or Uranus (who became the father who originated from Planet Uranus; and the Titan king of the Universe who sacrificed five of his children to the gods of his own understanding. However, Zeus was raised in secret and his mother was actually Kronos' sister, Rhea. He was spared by his evil father whom he later overthrew. This was history repeating itself because Kronos got into power by overthrowing his father. Again, pay very close attention:

12 Roman gods

1. Jupiter (king of the gods, sky and thunder). Jupiter is a stormy planet and its leader or Jove possessed the power of thunder and lightning.

2. Juno (queen of the gods, marriage and children)

3. Minerva (goddess of wisdom, war and craft)

4. Mars (god of war and violence)If you turn the letter 'M' upside down in the word Mars, you will get the word 'wars'. Basically, the name of this planet was war aka the planet of blood.

5. Venus (goddess of love, beauty and desire)

6. Apollo (god of the sun, music, poetry and prophecy)

7. Diana (goddess of the hunting, wilderness and childbirth)

8. Mercury (messenger god and god of commerce and travellers)

9. Ceres (goddess of agriculture and fertility)

10. Bacchus (god of wine, festivals and ecstasy)

11. Vulcan (god of fire, blacksmiths and volcanoes)

12. Vesta (goddess of health, home and family)

In addition, the Romans also worshipped leaders from other planets who had partnered to bring about Egypt's downfall.

Neptune (from Planet Neptune). He dwells in the sea. Remember, Planet Neptune, the eighth planet from the sun is known for its high content of water. So, yah. You can make your own mind up about this.

Pluto (from Planet Pluto). He dwells underground or in the underworld. Pluto is the darkest planet and the last of the nine planets that we came to know. It is dark and cold hence the reference to the underworld.

The other four appear on the list of gods and goddesses of Rome. They are Jupiter, Venus, Mercury and Mars. They all fought against Planet Earth. This then tells us about the power of the Black Headed Kings. It took more than nine leaders from other planets to defeat them.

So, yah. The number "12" has a sacred and deeper meaning and significance.

But why 12?

Remember; the structure of the Egypt that they were supposed to destroy was formed by 12 Black Headed Kings. However, their ranks and names were distorted by those who planned to defeat Egypt. Hence, according to the biblical narrative, they were made to appear as "gods" or they claimed to be gods who were brutal and evil. However, that was not the case and yet another lie about Africa.

Take a look at this structure below which built and formed a congregation of kings (not gods) of Egypt. All of them were labelled as kings, no matter what their gender was. They, along with our forefathers, formed the leadership structure in the Africa of ancient times. It was these eras which confused other humanoids from outer Earth about what was going on in Egypt. In actual fact, every man in Ancient Egypt was considered a king and a woman was known as a queen. This means that their children were princes and princesses by default.

Later, this was used against Egyptian kings and citizens by numerous enemies from different worlds. It was them who changed the narrative and lied that in Egypt there were more than 2,000 gods and goddesses. This is because the leaders of these alien alliances had a different perception of leadership. They believed that, like them, those who were leadership must be a god. Hence, they viewed the Black Headed Kings and the citizens of Egypt as gods.

However, whether or not they were gods, I'd like you to compare the structure of leadership that was put in place in Ancient Egypt by Amen Ra. This is the very structure that inspired these other enemy groups to use the number "12" when forming their own leadership structures. This made this number significant to them as well as their enemies.

Okay, let's see.

The 12 Kings of Egypt

These were pharaohs or faros and they originated from the moon.

1.   Amen Ra (sun king and the lord of all kings)

2. Isis (a female king who was considered as the mother king and king of magic and fertility)

3. Osiris (king of the afterlife and resurrection)

4. Anubis (king of mummification and protection)

5. Horus (king of kingship and protection)

6. Nephthys (A female king who was king of death and mourning)

7. Set (king of chaos and deserts)

8. Nuit (king of the night sky). She was a female king, hence the moon's purpose is to help fight the dark matter which comes with evil creatures.

9. Geb (king of the earth)

10. Nut (a female king who was king of the cosmos)

11. Thoth (king of wisdom, writing and magic)

12. Ma'at (a female king who was king of truth, justice and balance)

I'm not in favour of the Egyptian kings but their structure seems organic to me. As you can see, they had control over various things but nature and the cosmos were the most important areas of focus.

This was the structure that was copied by the Titans, the Annunaki group and the likes of the creatures from Europa, one of the moons of Jupiter. As a matter of fact, after forming what we know as Christianity, Illuminati and many other related cultures or should I say, "religions" and cults, their offspring questionably "decided" to use the name of Amen Ra, the enemy of their own gods. They used the name as a "locking word" in all their prayers. Why?

After all, they could have used the name of any of their numerous gods. How about Jupiter or Zeus? No, they chose to use Amen at the end of every prayer.

Why? To me, it is like when you use your enemy's power to become powerful yourself. It is like using your enemy's Nokia phone charging device to charge your Samsung phone. I know it sounds stupid but I think it's something like it.

Look, they all knew who the actual leader of Earth was. They knew that deep down in their conscious and they still do.

There could never be anything done without mentioning Amen Ra's name being mentioned in their affirmations.

Because, like I said, aliens are some kind of creature and a lot of work was done to and for Earth by the moon (the moon being more of a spaceship of its kind itself). This included what their spaceships couldn't do including the gravitational force, the kinetic energy and the radiocarbon that the moon produces for Earth to experience tidal power. This causes ocean tides and can be used to generate electricity. Ocean currents and circulation play crucial of a role in global climate regulation and marine ecosystems. It also ensures stabilisation of Earth's axis to maintain a constant climate. The moon has also been used for navigation and timekeeping for thousands of years along with creating calendar systems. There are many other interesting functions of the moon in addition to the four crucial abovementioned.

These were "sacrifices" made by the moon to Earth long before the Titans and the like came into the picture on this planet. And, I didn't hear anything about volcanoes, violence, the wilderness and earthquakes from the rank structure that was introduced to Earth by the Egyptian kings.

I only heard about all the organic stuff like protection, cosmos, writing, truth, justice and balance. I suppose these were needed on Earth.

So, I hope you can now see where I am coming from with the understanding of the moon and *Izinyanga* (later known as traditional healers). I hope you now understand why I said most of these creatures were called by the names of their planets or worlds of origin. For example, Pluto being called God Pluto, god of the underworld.

However, what this is about is to showcase the significance of what was set to be our living systems and how structured the life we live was. This was before the gods of Christianity invaded Earth and hacked our brains to get us to believe that they are gods. The kingship and protection that the Black Headed Kings of Egypt needed to be systematic and logical in order to live. It was these kinds of inputs that added value to the existence on Planet Earth and the presence of the faros or the pharaohs (the Black Headed Kings). Yes, these were not creatures of this world but they helped improve the lives of our forefathers in an organic manner because they had great concern for our ecosystem.

So, this could be the reason why today Earth is experiencing imbalances because of the greed and selfishness of the so-called gods of Christianity. The cut is deeper than just religion. However, religion would always reflect in our conversations because that was the tool that the evil gods of Christianity used to gain power and control over man. The Bible was their silver bullet to open the doors to our hearts, minds and eventually our souls.

They started by destroying the source of all of Earth's essential systems which are beyond man's understanding and the delicate balance of our ecosystem, for that means life in itself.

But, I think it's high time we expose the truth about what Christianity is, especially after the damage it has done to the livelihoods of the most notable people on Earth, the AbaNgoni.

We need to speak the truth about the damage it has done to rescue those who have been affected by such lies. It has turned our brothers, sisters, mothers, fathers and grandparents into mindless thinkers or zombies if you like. This is what I call a payless "self-sacrifice" into madness.

It is time we deal with this issue carefully and openly. If we don't future generations will fall for these stupid tricks from the darker space which are not easy to see.

The souls of masses are captured and their brains are controlled through the devices of Masonic Mind Control. They are enslaved into destroying the lands together with the bodies in which they belong and dwell within. To some of us, it's a disgrace to see them suffer for no particular gain but those of their pastors or priests and their "known" god whom they don't even know but worship him in ignorance.

Speaking of "worship", this is yet another word which was transformed in ensuring that its meaning was spared for the few. The word is derived from "warship" and this explains itself.

A warship is designed for combat in military operations. They are known for their ability to defend themselves from the enemy by being well equipped with weapons, armour etc. This is just like the church.

A warship is headed by a captain. This is similar to a church where the priest is in charge to help conduct the terms and conditions of the "worship" or "fellowship" and to instil the Gospel (God's spell) while channelling souls towards the darker space. This is similar to how a captain of a warship would channel his crew towards war.

Some priests who are scholars of the Bible believe they are at war with Satan. Little do they know that they are serving him every Sunday and some on a daily basis, simply because people don't pay enough attention to what they are doing. This is also the case when they read verses in the Bible and claim that they are reading with "understanding"

But perhaps, you'll need to read more about this well-covered story behind the Romans conflicting story of Jesus. Well, did you know that Horus, the Egyptian king, who was also known as The Light or the Son of the Sun, was a born of a virgin on 25 December? He started performing miracles at the age of 12, he had 12 friends and was later crucified and rose. That's not Jesus I'm talking about here but Horus.

Did you know about him? But, wait just a minute because there's actually more figures like Jesus who shared the same life as Horus. It was Horus who was the first of them all to have ever existed in this fashion. It is a very confusing and questionable fashion because this kind of an incident (whatever it was) occurred amongst several individuals from various cultures and religions and from different timelines and countries. However, Rome was unlike any other place. They would stop at nothing. Well, apparently they're said to have had this kind of weird experience twice because there's Mithra of Rome. She was born of a virgin on 25 December. She started performing magic, oops, I mean miracles at the age of 12, had 12 friends, was later crucified and resurrected.

Funny *ne*?

And I'm saying it's happened to Romans twice because it seems like stealing the Hebrew story of Horus. Oops! Pardon me. The story of Jesus wasn't enough.

The list of these similar characters goes on.

There's also Zoroaster, whose cult is even named after him, Zoroastrians. This is like Buddha of Buddhism, Krishna of Hindus, Dionysus of Greeks and then Attis of the Phrygian's belief system. All of these figures shared similar lives and deaths to those of Jesus. However, each of them made a different impact. This should widen our thoughts about who Jesus really was. Questioning your own religion is religious on its own, especially if what you truly want is religion. You better question it so you get answers before you waste any more time.

However, the number "12" keeps popping up. It must be making you curious about its relevance. Surely, there must be something.

Do you remember the story of the 12 sons of Jacob? This is confusing because Jacob did not mention his 13th child, his daughter Dina. Rather, he only uplifted his 12 sons.

Also, do you remember that after Judas betrayed Jesus, he was replaced by Matthias to ensure that there were still 12 apostles?

Later, the jury of every high court also appeared in a structure of 12 senior members in its deliberating body. But no, it doesn't end there. Some temples and religious organisations have a group of 12 senior members or leaders who often play highly decorated roles in their administration, spiritual guidance and decision-making processes of these structures. See examples below:

Freemasonry: Their Masonic temples or lodges have a council of 12 senior members known as the Twelve Apostles (does this ring a bell?) or Twelve Original Patrons. They oversee the temple's activities. Remember, this is a satanic cult.

Buddhist temples: The Buddhist temples also consist of 12 senior members known as the 12 senior monks or nuns. They are there to help guide the community and are also involved in decision-making processes in the temple.

Hindu temples: They're also said to have 12 senior members known as the *Dvadasha* or 12 trustees who are there to help manage the temples.

Mormon temples: In the Church of Jesus Christ of Latter-day Saints (LDS Church), each temple has its own presidency of three members who are then assisted by 12 senior members known as the Twelve Apostles (ring any bells?) or Twelve Matrons.

Later, we had a calendar of 12 months.

Oh! Now I think we're getting "hot", aren't we? Even the word "month" is derived from the word moon.

See, the moon is becoming significant once again. This is just like Amen Ra who has become so significant to even his enemies, the destroyers of Egypt themselves. Hence, all "satanic" or "evil" (666) organisations including the "Christian prayers" are still using his name "Amen" to lock their prayers.

Why? Why, if Egypt was a bad place and Amen Ra (of the moon) was evil? But his name still becomes very important at the end of your prayers as a Christian. This is said to be righteous but Amen Ra wasn't as per the narrative from your priests and pastors.

Why?

It doesn't make sense to me why Egypt was viewed as an evil place and its king brutal, yet we continue to use his name in prayers. This is just madness!

Can you make sense of this? Because, trust me I can't. I think Christians need to stop, think and redo their lives. They've been walking in the dark for a very long time and it's time they cast off the dark and begin travelling in the light and begin doing things as they should be done. By "light", I'm actually talking about the truth.

Okay, maybe this will help:

Revelation 12:9

" And the Great Dragon was thrown down, the serpent of old who is called the devil and Satan, the deceiver of the whole world; he was thrown down to the earth and his angels were thrown with him. " ...

Revelation means to show or prevail what is hidden, to reveal. Hence the Biblical word "revelation".

But, what does this verse tell you? Apart from the junk that priests are telling you.

Hmm! We need to be very realistic now. Time is moving guys.

Look, we need to understand that the Bible is a book and books are written by writers. As a writer, I'm going to ask this very important question (don't worry, I'm going to ask it on your behalf too). How and why would a "writer" who was intending to reveal something use words which were not exact? Like demons instead of angels because from where I'm standing, I remember angels being on God's side and not Satan?

Firstly, in the manner that I understand writing, a writer may not use words that he/she never intended to use.

Secondly, that was supposed to be a book of revelations, wasn't it? And the last I checked, to this date, when you're in the process of revealing something (unlike hiding it), you'd prefer using the "correct set of words" and "phrases" which are "exact or direct" than indirect words to help reveal what's needs to be revealed. That's not just a book of revelation but it is truly a book that was meant to reveal who Satan is.

Okay, perhaps repeating the verse would be useful:

Revelation 12:9

"And the Great Dragon was thrown down, the serpent of old who is called the devil and Satan, the deceiver of the whole world; he was thrown down to the earth and his angels were thrown with him.**"**...

Well, let's unpack this:

I'll start with the third word from the sentence or verse, "Great". In the context of someone's name, "great" is typically a positive gesture and epithet, an indication of_honour and admiration, a symbol of respect and recognition (regularly) of their achievements, qualities or impact of this given but highly decorated figure or person. It is also often used to signify that the person has made a significant contribution, demonstrated exceptional leadership or exhibited remarkable characteristics, etc.

Well, that was only "great" from "Great Dragon."

For example:

"And the Great Dragon was thrown down, the Great Serpent of old who is called the Great Devil and Satan, the deceiver of the whole world..." That's what the "great" in the verse stands for.

Now, I'd like us to look at the second but interesting series of words being used above, given their praising gesture "great" belted around each of them. This is to show you how admired the Great Deceiver of the whole word (as they label him) was by the writer. As the verse continues:

Example:

"...he was thrown down to the earth and his angels were thrown with him."

Okay, I'll begin with "his", which in its simplest of terms and context is to prove a strong sense of "ownership. For example, "his car", "his wife" or "his demons", etc.

And then, "angels" who are typically considered to be on God's side. But, who or what are angels?

Angels are spiritual beings. They don't have physical bodies. And their purpose is said to obey God's commands, carry out divine tasks and missions, uphold God's will and purposes, protect and guide God's people and oppose evil and darkness.

That's what angels are for, right? But, the Book of Revelation proves it all wrong! What do you say about that?

I know your priest will tell you nonsense that the version of angels used specifically in that verse meant demons because it is associated with Satan, right? I know that's what they will say.

But that's not true, because this was to reveal the truth, especially to those who are seeking the truth.

Here's another verse that is often misinterpreted by priests:

Psalm 111:10

" The fear of the Lord is the beginning of wisdom, all those who practice it have a good understanding. His praise endures forever! "

And then on a misinterpreted version of this verse, the priest would work on the fear as he's going to change it and replace it with a completely different word, "Respect".

People, fear and respect are two completely different words, especially to a writer. It may not be the case for the reader but writers choose the words for their readers to read.

From a writer's point of view, the writer wouldn't have used this word "fear" if what he meant was "respect". That's another thing you need to learn about "writing" than "speaking". The two get to vary because when one writes, the first thing they're worried about is whether or not their message will be heard. These then automatically makes a writer to rather want to stick to using a carefully selected set of words. This is vital in getting their message across because they know they won't be there when readers read through their work and to help elaborate where needs be. So, to avoid being misinterpreted and misunderstood, a writer would typically call a spade a spade!

Because what he intended to have written in their sentence or paragraph was actually "fear" and not "respect". It's not like there's no word such as "respect" in the Bible. There is. I hear a lot about obeying in many verses in the Bible and it's fitted where it's needed most. So people must stop acting as though they're not hearing what their Bibles are saying.

The word "fear" also needed to be fitted when the writer thought it was suitable to get their message across. I'm not sure if you understand me here.

But, don't worry because you don't have to. What you need to do is to open your bible and read the verses for what they are and for what they truly mean. Read the message and understand what it means to you. Don't change it for anything. It is exactly like what I have written in this book. It doesn't need to be changed for any particular reason whatsoever. Because once you do so, you'd literally be "overlooking" what I have written and perhaps even "questioning" my thoughts. This is not necessary. Instead, what you should do is question your own thoughts.

One thing that you should know about me is that I am not the person who writes what he doesn't mean. This explains the kind of writer I am.

And then we look at the word "endure" in the verse of Psalm 111:10 above. It means "to tolerate something unpleasant".

And as the writer ensures at the end of that sentence that "forever" this toleration must last.

Where is the good in that?

People, please just do not follow into something you don't even understand and be even aggressive and play ignorant when you're being told about it as evil. If you can't explain it, don't call it yours.

Because people act as though Christianity was designed by their family members as if they know it like the back of their hands. No, the majority of the Christian community is built by a group of individuals who literally do not understand anything about all that they "claim" they know and believe in.

However, I don't blame them. That's what the power of Masonic Mind Control does to brains. It weakens them!

These are the spiritual devices used to turn brains into enemies of their owners. That's why the biblical scholars were carefully instilled with "fear". Christianity makes it a point that fear becomes the basis or the foundation of its cult

They use fear to work on you. That's because you're easily controllable when you are "fearful" than when you're "brave" and "confident" about who you are.

Trust me, in everything that I am saying, I am not trying to disregard the presence of the "Higher Power" of my own understanding, *uMvelingqangi,* who was and still is the figure to which our spiritual power and understanding of the divine was adopted. They are the orders by which our forefathers lived. They were all in alignment with the understanding of who and what *uMvelingqangi* was about. Hence, it was believed that he was against evil and that is why they called themselves AbaNgoni (those who do not sin). There's enough evidence that proves that our forefathers "knew" about the existence of the Higher Power or the Divine. They knew this like the back of their hands, unlike many not knowing what Christianity stands for and where it belongs while they claim that they belong to it.

That's very dangerous. It's like loving someone you don't know what is it that they love, including yourself. This is very dangerous!

But, what I find even more organic about my forefather's way of viewing things is that they possessed a great sense of wisdom rather than education.

They knew that *uMvelingqangi* loved them. The understanding of that is found in the manner in which they decided to title him. The name says it all. They referred to him as "He who appeared first".

So, they already knew that he loved them so much that he appeared first. However, instead of making it to be something or someone else to belong to Earth, he decided to create them first among any other life forms or humanoids. This made a meaningful difference to them as it does to me.

Believe me, it doesn't get more organic, fair and genuine than that.

And yes later; for some reason, many AbaNgoni people lost meaning to this understanding, let alone the name *Mvelingqangi*.

So, it was these kinds of belief systems that the AbaNgoni people became a threat to the alien alliances and their plan of taking over Planet Earth. This made our forefathers feared for they knew what was beyond the concept of God that they landed with from their spaceships. That's what we today know as though it is, while there's actually nothing like it.

I'm so sorry you had to find out this way but there's nothing like one God or one who doesn't possess a physical body like me and you. According to alien understanding, the concept of god is a figure that they could see or touch. Such individuals would be honoured with the title of "god" or "goddess" given the unique abilities and strength they possessed through their bloodline. That's who the creatures of the moon understood as being Lord rather than "God".

That's what God or who God was and still is to them, a figure they would be able to touch as they offer sacrifices. And now that's what and who God is or is understood as being by you. Because many nowadays are believed to be living with their own gods in their own homes for wealth and power purposes.

This is unlike *uMvelingqangi* (the Higher Power of my own understanding) who was unseen and untouched by none of our forefathers. It was them who revealed this powerful and remarkable knowledge and understanding (in the form of teachings) about his supernatural presence which was and still is unseen and untouched, except in seeing or touching another Ngoni being. This is unlike the many different forms of AbaNgoni mimics, beings who were "made" rather than created, such as your "mankind", "humankind", "human beings", etc.

So, I hope you still recall what narrative has brought us this far or maybe this deep. But don't worry, I do.

We were speaking of *Izinyanga*, creatures or humanoids from the moon who played a huge role in Kwa-Bantu— the land of the Ngoni people and where the wider community of AbaNgoni people came from.

This is especially about those who existed then and this has caused great confusion over time about who those creatures were.

That's because their story has been robbed of its own meaning and its own history. It was never documented in the first place. There's a lot we need to know about our lives, which includes the lives of our forefathers and the things we may not be able to change about their lives as opposed to our lives.

Some of our forefathers, to whom we are nothing without, used to be in contact with some of the creatures from the moon, such as *Izinyanga*. The name *Izinyanga* remains and not gods. They taught our forefathers about leadership and kingship. They were actually what people today call *Amadlozi* (ancestors) as opposed to *Abathonga* (those who fell asleep).

However, because this new way of believing was one which was "unusual" and its rituals were practiced in the mountains (*eKuphakameni*) and usually in the darker hours of the day, it was questionable by many of our forefathers. Some believed and even called it *Ingozi* (danger), a word which was later transformed when written and appeared as *Idlozi*. However, you get to know the truth about this when you get to hear about the likes of a spiritual upheaval or a weird moment if you may, that was and still likely to occur to someone who's known to possess *Idlozi* called *Amadlingozi*. It is a short way of saying *Amadla Ingozi* (those who had consumed danger).

This phrase is the evidence of what I mean by *Idlozi*, a word or name being derived from *Ingozi*. Because as much as the newer races may have wanted to erase the ancient Ngoni language; they wouldn't have managed to entirely change how people spoke because not all of them were interested in reading or learning how to read. So, some words were transformed but some got to be preserved in the language of AbaNgoni.

For instance, the phrase *Amadlingozi* which was believed to be something that people would normally do when possessed by *Amadlozi* (ancestors) which back then would normally be the creatures of the moon (*Izinyanga*) or ancient water beings who were called *Amandambhi*.

However, the phrase *Amadlingozi* still exists in a world where the AbaNgoni language has been changed into isiZulu language.

The person who's considered to be possessed with this would normally react exactly like someone who's said to be possessed with demons and can be very dangerous and even deadly. This is especially around people who may not know what needs to be done to calm them down or get them back to normal. They'd act all weird and abnormal — crazy! If I may, like a mad person, they'd say and do things as if they are communicating with the invisible figures of some sort. This is highly possible because there's a process of *uKuthwala* that some people with these reactions would involve themselves with. These are often deep and sacred yet secret rituals said to be influenced by the voodoo tradition or cult.

I think we need to unpack the process of *uKuthwala* and see what we can find. These kinds of operations are to prepare you for the upcoming conversations about our heritage, not only as the Malinga family but as the entire emaSwati tribe in general. You will be amazed to find out that we have come a very long way in life.

So; what is it meant by *uKuthwala*?

That is a good question! Well. without wasting our already wasted time, I shall go straight into it.

uKuthwala was a process practiced in ancient times. Like I mentioned, there were a number of alien creatures from other worlds who later invaded Earth in much higher volumes. But first, as I mentioned, these deeply spiritual practices or operations were first conducted by the creatures from the moon (*Izinyanga*), apart from the kings of Egypt themselves. That's because their kingship was formed by different creatures including those from the sun.

However, the *Izinyanga* were a true ancestry of the kings of Egypt. They wouldn't have gained access to the moon without having to pass through the jury of 12 *Izinyanga* who are actually the origins of the bloodline of the kingship of the moon itself therefore, Earth. This means that nothing goes without their authority on Earth.

Unlike the kings of Egypt who lived in palaces, they lived in the mountains. Each of them possessed a unique supernatural power. They showcased and displayed magnitudes amounts of magic and science combined in their unique doings. Hence, during the process of *uKuthwala* where both science and magic were used to wipe the older knowledge as they instilled new information, abilities and powers into people's bodies and brains in exchange for souls. This means that it was a process of exchanging souls, where a person would sacrifice theirs in return for the power of another of a different species. These were conducted as per the purpose measured to be performed by the candidate who was undergoing this process of *uKuthwala*.

A good example would be in the early stages. It would be the souls of alien creatures like lions, cats, wolves, bats, owls, snakes and many other animals which were used in the process of *Ukuthwala*. Any of these spirits would then be a supplement to a person's sacrificed soul. This person's life changed completely. Some would do this to acquire wealth, fame and power.

So, if what was used upon you during this process was a snake, you'd then possess the powers and the magical abilities of snakes too, including to react and/ or transform into one when the time comes (whenever that is). You may have heard of people who would normally transform into cats when their enemies were searching for them while others would turn into birds and fly away.

These were powers that were intended for people who were interested in having them. This means that the *Izinyanga* were powerful creatures.

They were the ones to go to when you were interested in acquiring these powers. However, no one could enter the homes of *Izinyanga* which were located in caves in the mountains. The mountains were once known as ancient houses of the lords (alien creatures). Our fore-fathers knew these mountains as *Ekuphakameni* (the higher ground). Many of them were made by giants to accommodate creatures of other worlds, Hence, different mountains possess different vibrations caused by the impact of the components and elements used to build them. This includes rocks, metals, slaving animals and insects. It also includes water and the kind of soils that allowed these creatures to grow certain plants from their planet of origin. All of this together was responsible for producing the kind of environment and gases these creatures are used to.

Some creatures from the moon lived in the waters. These were the ones believed to have been gushed down to Earth together with the seas of our moon.

That is another but untold story of the sacrifice that the moon offered to Earth to maintain the radio-carbon energy and gravitational force. It is because of this water sacrifice from the moon that Earth's seas have rivers and lakes that feed into them.

So, the water from the moon brought another species of creatures and humanoids who dwelled in the waters. This is apart from mermaids (who were magically and scientifically made by the goddess of Greece, Athena). I am not referring to them. I am talking about creatures who lived amongst them such as *Amandambhi* and *Izilo-Zengubo*. These were water beings from the moon who were gushed down upon Earth together with the seas of the moon.

The likes of Jupiter and Venus copied the same method by raining down on Earth waters from their own planets, adding to the lakes and rivers infrastructure that Earth has today. However, these may have dwelled in two completely different environments; in the mountains and the waters but they possessed a similar gesture to Earth's life and other lives. They respected the nature of Earth and the people equally. They would also help our forefathers from time to time in gathering the smaller pieces of information about organically and spiritually improving their lives and about the necessary structures within life. Later, this led to our forefathers understanding traditional leaderships and monarchies. Hence, many would be said to have been to the waters or mountains to possess supernatural powers, including being wealthy and owning cattle.

However, before we spread even wider into the narrative of *uKuthwala*, while we are discussing water beings, it would be a good idea to talk about the competition amongst the water beings from the moon (*Amandambhi*). They were later ambushed by their equals, mermaids and many other water creatures, intent on taking over the power and spirit of the *Amandambhi.* However, what they desired most was their deep connection with the people of Earth, AbaNgoni.

Like I mentioned, these were manmade equals of *Amandambhi* and *Izilo-Zengubo.*

This war lasted for years and eventually the waters of Africa were filled with mermaids, many of them looked white or Indian. Unlike *Amandambhi,* these were more into manipulating people into certain beliefs and secret sacred operations such as satanic rituals rather than healing. They fed on flesh and blood. That is why people started to fear lakes and rivers as it was believed that they were associated with *Ingozi,* later *Idlozi.*

Here's an interesting one. It is believed that some of those creatures from the moon, *Amandambhi, Izilo-Zengubo* and *Izinyanya,* somehow but scientifically and magically transformed themselves into men and women who later joined our tribes and races.

They lived on land and some started enjoying their stay on the ground. However, some had to make lakes their own by using water from the moon. In this way, no other creature from another world could easily invade them.

So, this then tells us that different rivers and lakes possess waters that belong to different worlds and moons of the Universe. This also makes the creatures found in them different and come from different worlds.

The division or the spheres that form the different environments found on Earth are known as dimensions. It was the multiplication of those alien creatures from different worlds that created permanent division amongst us. Today, these aliens are secret but permanent citizens of Planet Earth.

Look, some of the things that happened in the past do sound like a myth or a joke sometimes. However, many of them are true but untold. Yes, there are many alien creatures who live on Earth.

Many years later, newer kinds of people with weird beliefs and different ways of living emerged throughout the so-called black community. Their physical appearances were different as some possessed features which were unusual. This includes Abathwa, Nyasa and Thonga or Tonga people, etc. who appeared very short but very powerful in nature. They knew all that AngaNgoni didn't know including foreseeing the future. They knew how plants could heal and protect people. These beings included the Nyasa (a name derived from Nyanga) and Thonga people (derived from Aba-Thonga) which means "those who have gone to sleep", referring to the dead. However, their identity on land was hidden. They wouldn't be called by their original names given the wars of the time but they were allied to the Ngoni group who were the only ones who knew the origin of these new people.

For instance, the Nguni naming of those tribes carried an understanding of whom those tribes were and where they were from. For example, Abathwa (derived from Abathwala) which also retraces us to those who conducted the *Ukuthwala* process being creatures from the moon.

All the names of these three tribes carried deep meanings in each of their contexts. As a matter of fact, they then became part of the Nguni group. However, they were respected for their unique and powerful differences.

Perhaps you are asking why I say these were creatures from the moon.

See, all three groups spoke completely different languages yet their names were derived from the Ngoni language. Why? Like the creatures of the moon, they also had a close relationship with the Ngoni people. Hence, the Amathonga or Thonga or Tonga people were widely scattered as the AbaNgoni people were. You'd find them in Tanzania, Zambia, Zimbabwe, Namibia and Mozambique. Later, just like the Ngoni group, some were found in the Kwazulu-Natal region in a place called Kwamhlaba Uyalingana.

This secret was kept by *Amakosi* (the kings), which was where the sacred rituals of kingship of the moon were practiced in secrecy.

I have mentioned earlier that the creatures of the moon had a deep connection with nature. The same can be said for the Nyasa, Thonga and Abathwa. That is why they were later known for the herbs, *uKuthaka,* for healing or killing purposes.

Hence, the word *uButhakathi* was derived from *uButhaka* or *uButhakathaka,* a word referring to someone who's ill or not feeling very well. This person would then need *uKuthakwa,* the process of *muthi* (plant) or herb-mixing and applying and consumption by the sick..

All these words are mothered by a simple word — *isithako* meaning "ingredient". This means that there were *muthi* ingredients aimed at healing or killing something or someone. This was later described as *uButhakathi,* which generally means all which is bad or even evil.

However, these were words that lost their meaning over time. The meanings of these words explain that these were people who knew the correct plants for almost everything that was troubling man. This was generally called *uButhakathi* (medical practitioner).

However, this didn't only refer to man like AbaNgoni (our forefathers).

As peaceful as they seemed, they were not an easy group to fight against and defeat. They were too magical for that. These were groups who carried a thunder and lightning bolt and some of them were water and air benders. As short as they were, they defeated giants. They also had the ability to disappear into thin air during battle.

As a result, our forefathers had no choice but to let them join the AbaNgoni group and become part of us. They also played a big role in ensuring that AbaNgoni people were respected, feared and recognised as dangerous. And that's what our forefathers wanted in the first place.

However, I don't want to talk much about that, especially in this book. Rather, I will explain *Ukuthwasa* as opposed to *Ukuthwala*.

So, why waste time? Let's dive into it once and for all. Look, like I may have mentioned those who went through the process of *Ukuthwala* were actually a group of people who chose the process for themselves. However, the *Ukuthwasa* or *Ukuthweswa* or *Ukwethweswa* process would actually be a process where a person would be chosen by the creatures of the moon themselves, the likes of *Amandambhi* (who dwelled in the waters), *Izinganga* (who dwelled in the mountains) or *Izilo-Zengubo* (water and land beings). They were chosen according to a particular bloodline.

Ukuthwala is a Ngoni word meaning "carrying or to carry". This means that these people who went through the process of *uKuthwala* or *uKwethweswa* by either their own will or that of the creatures of the moon actually entered into a similar trend, a similar frequency or perhaps a similar "ritual". This means that whatever they carried was of the same fashion.

However, the difference between a person who's from the processes of *uKuthwala* and *uKwethweswa* or *uKuthwasa* is that the one from the *uKuthwala* process may have done it for their personal gain, while the other one from the *uKuthwasa* process may have been chosen to perform a particular duty or duties of the creatures of the moon (also known as *Amakhosi*). This would mostly be in return for healing powers, the power to foresee the future, etc.

To tell you the truth, this was a very interesting find that I discovered while searching for the truth. The truth behind AbaNgoni's life and the truth about what we today know as "evil" and what we know as "righteous". I personally think we may find balance in exploring the two. In my understanding, the truth is what will set us all free.

That's because not knowing the truth about what you claim you hate or dislike is pointless. You might as well begin loving it. You have no reason to hate what you don't know and this applies to love. You need to know what it is that you love. Not only does it feel good to love but it must also make sense, as much as you'd still need to make sense of what you love or hate.

That's because what happened in our lives was actually a sad thing as we kept on joining operations we didn't fully understand. We basically followed what was done without questioning it. That's why people are angry at themselves because many are so frustrated with the delays in changing their current situations after a long walk of worshipping. They simply practice what their given cults, cultures and religions order them to do.

We have forgotten that our purposes vary from one person to the next. Some of you weren't supposed to follow a religion or be in a cult. However, some were meant for these kinds of operations because not all of us are Ngoni people anymore — anyway! Some of us developed from the cluster of newer groups that were mushrooming throughout the land. That's why we're not the same in spirit because our souls and therefore purposes are not of the AbaNgoni people. This means that our doings and ways of living may never be of the same fashion. Some are seeking the truth while some are seeking the lie. Each one finds themselves in their own space. It always comes back to different strokes for different folks.

I like the fact that there is truth that can never be shaken by anything. It's the bottom line of almost everything. The truth speaks of "purposes" as the nature of our differences in our beings. And the truth says we are to focus on what we can and leave behind what we cannot.

So, I'm only doing what I can to document some of the things that we need to know and understand about life or what has been displayed as life when it's just the opposite of what we think it is.

In the mind of a philosopher nothing is as bad as it seems. It all depends on how our brains function towards reality and how we get to shift our thoughts or perspectives around what is from what isn't, especially for our individual point of interest.

What we consume should be in alignment with our purpose; our purpose being our souls who are guided from time to time by the gods of our own understanding, whether we want to or not. That's because some of these "deals" were made possible by our forefathers and some were made possible by our nature and origins being different from one another. Not every one of us comes from the same source and that is the life of Earth, despite our families being the same or whether or not we belong to the same parents.

It is a sad reality that our purpose belongs to different sources and they originate from different spheres.

Moving right on...

In this chapter, we're exposed to some of the things that may sound weird or even impossible to have ever happened. Because yes, in this world you live what you make sense out of. And it was this kind of freedom in life that ended up keeping other people "less free", because the more you learn about what is hidden in life, you get to be free. Like I mentioned, it was this kind of freedom that then later kept other people enslaved and made them see no glimpse of light of freedom. You would remember that we live in a world filled with evil song singers and evil song writers who are greedy to such an extent that the truth is reserved for a few individuals while the rest become nothing but slaves of misinterpreted information, leading them down the cliff without them knowing it.

That's why people will need to pay to regain their freedom because none of us were born slaves. We were all born free and none of us were born sinners. That's nonsense! And it's the kind of nonsense that was built against what our forefathers were, what they believed in and who they strongly believed they were not.

They were those who never sinned (AbaNgoni) and then later, when they were known as AbaNguni (a name without a meaning). They were taught that they were born sinners by the biblical study which was forced on them by whites.

Psalm 51:5

" Behold, I was brought forth in iniquity, and in sin did my mother conceive me. "

Psalm 58:3

" Even from birth the wicked go astray, from the womb they are wayward, spreading lies. "

Lol. "From the womb!? Spreading lies?" Are you kidding me?

Corinthians 2:14

" The natural person does not accept the things of the Spirit of God, for they are folly to him, and he cannot understand them, because they are spiritually discerned. "

So, these are the kinds of misleading information about life. It was not of our forefathers' will to adhere to this nonsense but they were forced into changing what they believed in. Those who resisted the so-called Word of God were brutally killed. They didn't have a choice.

This left those who feared for their lives no choice but to join Christianity where they were cornered to know what we know today and that is that we are a bunch of sinners. By knowing this, you automatically lose hope in your own life. You lose focus on doing what you know is right because whether or not you do the right thing, you are already a sinner anyway. This gives you the impression that life is just a wasteful exercise and too bad to be lived well. That's what this was about; you just need to be smart to see it.

Many people, including myself, were very confused by this narrative of the Bible because it also doesn't make sense, does it? Because a newborn baby has nothing to do with the sins of their folks. My understanding is that a newborn carries no sin. A sinner is someone who does bad or evil things! That's a sinner! So, what if no one in your family has ever committed any crime or sin? What is that called then? Are they still sinners?

This isn't logical to me, especially when a baby is meant to be a blessing but is still a sinner. I literally don't find sense in that but that's just my way of seeing it. And trust me, I like the fact that I was never a person who saw things through the eyes of the majority. Because that's how I get to find the truth. I find the truth in seeking for one in the midst of all that the majority isn't paying enough attention to. I read and gather information from all which is never said, especially by the majority.

My journey to join the pieces of the puzzle is caused by what our lives have become. It is by feeling lost because the more I learnt about the biblical stories, I felt that I was slowly losing the meaning of life, except for the one set by different biblical scholars (your priests and them). To me, some of them need direction themselves. They need to be true to themselves and look at things in life for what they truly are. Because there's no need to follow the belief systems of other people and look down on the one you should be adhering your faith to. It becomes very unfair to your *AbaThonga*.

I want to say something about this subject of *AbaThonga* because I think that's where we'll find clarity as to what the difference between them and *Amadlozi* are. These are the things that caused a huge division between the essence of understanding the other and the non-essence of the lack of understanding of the other. This, in its own, created division and tendencies of avoidance in what we should be exactly looking at. And, it is very important for us to look into what is dividing us as a people and find solutions.

From where I'm standing, people need to know what it is that they love as much as they understand what it is that they hate. That's because hating what you don't understand can be very dangerous and the same applies to loving what you don't understand.

Hence, I personally had to research deeper about what many people claim that they loved and what many people claimed that they hated most.

I don't want to be only a follower, but I also want to be a questioner as I follow. Before I find myself losing direction because I did something simply because everyone was doing it. I hate that. I'd rather lose direction because no one was travelling with me. This is what made me want to seek the truth about *Amadlozi* and religion or should I say traditions or culture and Christianity which are the greatest subjects of old instead of wanting to follow any of the two faculties without any valid reason.

I don't find peace in choosing sides in a battle that's dividing our families, rather, I must find a cure to its ending.

Look, we need to remember that *Amadlozi* are exactly like what we understand as angels and demons or generally aliens.

We need to be reminded of the presence of creatures from other worlds who invaded Earth a long time ago for us to change much now. What I'm saying here is that unlike *iThonga*, *iDlozi* lives. And the frequency that these angels or demons are likely to use to connect with us is similar. They use the same channel and that is magic and natural sciences beyond the man of Earth's (aBantu's) understanding.

These can also be looked at as "the fallen angels".

The Creator created Planet Earth and then our fore-fathers. There was no sin until the fallen angels who followed after the so-called sin of Adam and Eve.

They have nothing to do with the aBantu group but are part of the history of where Hebrew people originate from. Those were made rather than created. After all, that is what the Bible is about. It tells the history of the Hebrews and their gods or aliens to be precise. It is not the history of aBantu which doesn't appear as much in the books of the Bible. We don't get to hear about the names and places that we are used to or that should resonate with our history.

This then becomes questionable, not in the context of trying to be a Christian sceptic or agnostic. No, it is from the realistic point of view. As a matter of fact, if no one was forced and killed to believe in Christianity, I believe there would be very few AbaNgoni people who would have followed it.

Even the other name for God, Jahweh, is derived from Hebrew and not Ngoni. It means "He who is" or "The Self-Existent One" and we all know what "He, Who or One" means, right? But, wait a second!

Isn't this the very same understanding that our fore-fathers (the first to live on Earth, thousands of years before Hebrew people were made in Eden) had about *uMvelingqangi?* This was a figure which was not known nor referred to as any gender per se and which was believed to have been protecting the nation of AbaNgoni (aBantu) but from the context of a "spiritual provision and protection" point of view. Sure it is.

Okay, forget about that. Now, let's look at the name Jahweh which is somehow interchangeable with Jehovah for some reason. It is believed to be empha-sising God's eternal existence and covenant relation-ship with Israel (not South Africa). It has been used more than 6,800 times in the Old Testament.

Why? Because Jahweh was worshipped together with his wife, Goddess Asherah in the place of many gods of Israel. The existence of "The Queen of Heavens" is mentioned in Jeremiah 7:18 and Verse 44:17-19. In the Bible, it talks about worshipping one god and yet she earned the title of goddess. Imagine that. She got to be Goddess Asherah who was worshipped in Israel alongside who should have been known as God; which then points us back to Jahweh. And that's only if Jahweh was the only god. For there should have been one goddess then. I'm not sure if you understand this.

Okay, I think I'm moving too fast now. Let's take a step back because I meant to speak about the angels and the like. I hope you remember what brought us to this point. We were talking about the things that make me think that the history of the Bible and the god being mentioned there, as rich as it may sound, doesn't really resonate with the version of our own history and that of the understanding of what God was as opposed to who God wasn't to the AbaNgoni people. That's what got us here.

So yah! Angels.

Look, I know we all understand angels as good spirits or good guardians and all that but I also would like to highlight a thing or two about this very subject. This becomes my own opinion or my personal thoughts which are not affiliated with anyone else. I think we all know by now about the manipulation that has been done over us and what we all must be aware of. This should help us open our eyes a bit wider and look for anything that is holding us back and sure, we'll find some. Well, that's you because me, on the other hand, personally thinks that what's holding us back is the "thinking".

Should we begin "thinking" differently about the life that we were programmed to "think" that we're living all will be well. Because that's what is adding to the pile of problems that we have — and the major one is that of not being able to see what is "right" from "wrong". Because if you were taught that right is wrong, you'd kill anyone who'd try and change you from wrong to the actual right (which is not wrong).

A brain is one teachable phenomenon of an organ. It can be very awkward to change it from what it already knows. Hence, trying to adjust our thoughts would from time to time help us gain control over what we think or over our thoughts therefore, what we do. For our thoughts are highly likely to become things. This then means a set of bad thoughts are likely to lead us into bad situations, things, places or people. But, when you're not aware of how bad your thoughts are or can be, you may fail to learn whether or not certain places, things, people and situations are bad for you. This drives us backwards to "thinking" to what should be a shift in our thinking or thoughts. It is that right there that is holding us back as a people, especially the so-called black people.

These are the people whose lives were turned into some charity and case study of white people. Our lives are planned because the system is programmed to weaken our brains.

Okay, now let's speak about aliens. Oops! I meant to say angels. But, wait a minute! What's the difference between these two? To me, there's none. That's because they share a similar description and are both similar to what demons are also described to be. So, when does one know when they're dealing with any of these two? Say, demons, for instance.

Hmm! The reason why I'm asking this is because we need to be also aware of the evil angels or the ones which were cursed and thrown down to Earth. There are a lot of these creatures and some were not even documented in the Bible. They bombarded Earth over the years and after the Bible was published. As we speak, an alien ship or UFO is landing somewhere and they're bringing us more creatures from different worlds or from a different world. How do we know that they are not angels? Look, I'm trying to make sense out of this. I'm trying to be realistic also and trying to be fair in the process because I know for sure how sensitive this subject can be. We all know angels as good spiritual beings and who are here to help provide protection over our lives. They are our warriors of some sort. Well, think about it. If these were thrown down to Earth to protect us, how many of them are there that still live among us? Please, just play around these thoughts and maybe make up your own figures. As mentioned, I'm only trying to get some clarity here.

I know I may sound stupid or perhaps too narrow-minded to those who believe in angels. But, here's my narrative:

I think these two terms, demons and angels, were terms meant to distinguish the difference in nature of alien creatures.

Because yes, they were both cut from the same cloth. They are actually alien beings who had different missions on Planet Earth. This then means these were good and bad alien creatures whose lives were entitled to ours, given the orders of their leaderships of the worlds in which they all individually origi-nate. Even the book that made us know about angels mentions that they belonged to a different world from Planet Earth as it is mentioned that they were thrown down onto our lives together with the devil. Perhaps I should find us another verse where the book speaks of fallen angels.

Here's one and please read it carefully.

Isaiah 14:12-15

" How you have fallen from Heaven, morning star, son of the dawn! You have been cast down to the earth, you who once laid low the nations! You said in your heart, 'I will ascend to the heavens, I will raise my throne above the stars of God; I will sit enthroned on the mount of assembly, on the utmost heights of Mount Zaphon. I will ascend above the tops of the clouds; I

will make myself like the Most High.' But
you are brought down to the grave to the
depths of the pit. **„**

Okay, I hope you went through this verse thoroughly.
Now, I want us to look into it by breaking it down
so that we see the same picture as the writer, poor
Isaiah. His intention for documenting this must be
marked as genuine and meant to have gotten the
message clearly across. To me, the message must not
be distorted and should be understood for what it
truly means. Don't wait for your pastor to break it
down for you because it's very clear. It's not a verse
one should struggle to understand.

Okay, let's get down to business. I am going to repeat
the verse below because it is going to be carefully
broken down into many pieces until it starts to make
sense to us, just like it did to Isaiah. Poor Isaiah.

"How you have fallen from Heaven, morning star, son
of the dawn! You have been cast down to the earth,
you who once laid low the nations! You said in your
heart, 'I will ascend to the heavens, I will raise my
throne above the stars of God; I will sit enthroned
on the mount of assembly, on the utmost heights of
Mount Zaphon. I will ascend above the tops of the
clouds; I will make myself like the Most High.' But
you are brought down to the grave, to the depths of
the pit."

First, let's discuss "Heaven" before we explain about Isaiah. Heaven is said to be outside of this planet. I'll presume it's another planet then, right? Which then means the Bible agrees with me by saying, "Lucifer came from another world" and was cast down to the earth. That should be something very strange and for that matter questioned but it has not. Not because it came from the mouth of a priest, isn't it?"

And then; let's look at the short line, "son of the dawn" — the dawn being the beginning of light and we know Lucifer being related to the dark. Isn't this confusing already?

Especially in a world where the Illuminati group and Masonries speak of being enlightened or enlightenment and yet they perform their rituals in secrecy in the dark.

Okay, before I lose you, let's continue.

So, Isaiah labels or titles Lucifer "the son of the dawn". Why? Why would he want to call him this way as though he knew something that we didn't know about Lucifer and (the light)? That's because in the verse it is actually Isaiah who recognised Lucifer as the Morning Star or The Beginning of Light which is the "dawn". Yet, in the very same verse, Isaiah also displays the knowledge that Lucifer "was he who laid low the nations". This means "he slayed or killed and fatally defeated as he destroyed the nations". Because "laid low" is actually an idiomatic expression which can be very direct in terms of proving meaning. Yet, "laid low" can also have several meanings depending on the contexts in which it's utilised. We all know that Lucifer is represented as an evil figure, right? This means that "laid low" according to Isaiah meant killing and destroying nations.

If you know the Ngoni praises called *Izibongo,* you'd know what Isaiah was doing in saying, "He who laid low the nations." If I were to translate what this says into Ngoni language, it would go like this, *"Wena owalalisa uqaqa ezisweni".* And that's what Lucifer is known for — his brutality.

However, some would say Isaiah's "laid low" (quoted from Isaiah 14:12-15) was referring to Lucifer's downfall or falling down from Heaven. This becomes confusing because in the very same verse, Isaiah mentioned the part where Lucifer was brought down! He mentions this at the beginning of the verse and repeats it later.

"How you have fallen from Heaven" and he repeats, "You have been cast down to the earth." Does it even ring any bells?

So yah! I think I'll leave this one to you. Now, I'd like us to discuss the part where Isaiah mentions the desire that Lucifer had in his heart, where he says, "I will ascend to the heavens." Well, did Isaiah know what was in Lucifer's heart? But yah, That's what Isaiah says was in Lucifer's heart, "to actually ascend (to rise) to the heavens".

And he does what?

Well, behold as it will still become interesting. So, it looks like our guy here was looking forward to rising back to the heavens where he desired to "raise his throne above the stars of God; and I sit enthroned on the mount of assembly," he says.

Well, not only did Lucifer want to ascend to the heavens but he also wanted to sit on his throne. Thrones are meant for kings and queens, aren't they? This means that he was still "King". Correct me if I'm wrong because here's Isaiah saying it in his book that Lucifer wanted to rise with his "throne" and sit "Eenthroned"! Okay, wait a minute right there now Isaiah while I try and break down this word "enthroned" and unpack it nicely for us so that we're on the same page. I'd like us to look into the powerful and rich message that it carries.

Enthroned can actually emphasise several expressions of dominion or power given its multiple facets which are all powerful in symbolism. It is also believed that it means to be exalted or worshipped as either king or queen or to sit on a throne or a ceremony to mark the beginning of the rule of a king. Basically, enthronement conveys protection and provision, wisdom and justice, majesty and glory, authority and dominion.

And there's a part that mentions Mount Zaphon as the Mount of Assembly. Well, the last I heard this phrase, "Mount of Assembly" it was on a documentary I once watched about the Illuminati group. The documentary was about exposing the secret lives of Illuminati members and the disadvantages of joining the organisation. And, a certain portion of it would then narrate a tale of the Mount of Assembly as a secret and sacred place — which is where members of their organisation would gather annually to "worship" and offer a "blood sacrifice" to the gods of their organisation who dwell in this Mount of Assembly.

But, now, the question is: Who is the leader of this empire, Mount Zaphon, also known as Heaven?

Trust me, you don't want to know, okay? Because, yes, the Book of Isaiah made it all sound as though the Mount of Assembly was a good place to have been invaded by Lucifer for that matter.

But you'll be shocked as to who was and still is the leader of Mount Zaphon, a place known to be the connector of Heaven and Earth, simply Heaven.

Well, it was ruled by Baal!

Baal is actually one of a couple of so-called gods found in the structure of deities (the likes of Dagon, Baphomet, Morloch, etc.) who are worshipped secretly in the Illuminati organisation. They are a gigantic satanic cult dating from the 16th century. It was founded and funded by the descendants of Jacob — the 12 Tribes of Israel. This is where Baal becomes second after Morloch in terms of their ranks. They are highly significant figures of this "evil" organisation.

Baal is often confused with Lucifer however, they are actually different figures. Unlike Lucifer, Baal is said to be "the king of the gods" as well as the god of fertility, weather and war. He is the son of El or Zaphon himself (known as the chief god), "father of the gods" or "god of creation and wisdom". He was the ruler of the Divine Assembly (where blood sacrifices are offered). Illuminati members would call it the Divine Assembly (a place where their gods would magically receive their sacrifices or offerings etc.).

However, there was also a figure known as Hadad known to be a "storm god". He would occasionally visit the Mount of Assembly but Anat (Baal's sister), Athtar (god of the Morning Star) and Shapash (goddess of the sun) were always found in the Mount of Assembly as the trusted deities of the cult. This place, according to Isaiah, was considered to be Heaven.

Lucifer desired and envied to be the one to whom all those blood sacrifices were and are still offered to. It appears that he desired to be like the Most High. It's believed that many famous and wealthy actors, sports people, singers, politicians and presidents and many important (so-called) members of this world, especially the ones considered as celebrities and idols worship these gods (which are also indirectly used by Isaiah by mentioning Mount Zaphon). So, this then means a lot of blood sacrifice is done there annually. But wait, we're not done yet. Who is your god amongst all these deities?

Okay, I'm done now but only with Isaiah's revelation, which is a mouthful. However, to someone whose intention is to seek the truth because this verse does not say what it tells me to everyone. Some are hearing what becomes their priests' interpretation around it, which is shielded with layers of manipulation and betrayals of different shapes, sizes and colours.

When I tell people that both Christianity and the Illuminati are adopting orders from a similar source of power, wisdom and strength to manipulate as many people as possible, the Christians won't hear it. This is caused by Masonic Mind Control used by the leaders of the Temples and Lodges of these great institutions, Christianity and Illuminati. And what makes these two institutions great? It's us, the people who are seeking power elsewhere than from themselves.

By searching how our forefathers lived is like searching deeper inside your own pockets than searching inside someone else's pocket. Because, looking at how our forefathers lived may truly do wonders for our lives. It is then and only then we shall be able to look deeper into ourselves.

Look, this may sound like an insult because it's true. The majority of us do have some skin cuts called *Izingcabo* on our bodies. The word is derived from a Ngoni word *uKugcaba*; dating from an ancient era when *Usiko* (skin cutting) was practiced. The process is connected with *Usiko* which is never a word to symbolise or define culture, but it was just another era.

However, these weren't only practiced to hide one's identity but it also entailed numerous reasons why it was performed. This includes strength and protection from enemies, prevention and cure for unforeseen dangers and illnesses, and power.

Some would undergo this process of *uKugcatshwa* or *uKugcaba* to enhance and balance their chakras and spiritual realms (which is power on its own). The process would generally be called *uKuqiniswa* or *uKuqina*(meaning strengthened). Some would perform it for wealth and fortune. As much as some of these processes may have used in a similar style (which was to cut skins) they each entailed different *muthi* herbs, *Izithako* (ingredients) usually known as *Izinsizi* or *Insizi* used right after the skin was cut. This is when the *muthi* mix is applied to the open wound or cut to allow it to run through the blood. For whatever purpose it may have been done for, be it protection, power or wealth, the *muthi* or *Insizi* would do exactly as it was ordered. But then, not all clans would do what is mentioned above. To some, it was a combination of factors.

I am sure you remember the name *Amabhaca* derived from a Swati word for "hiding" (*uKubhaca*). Hence, I mention that some would do these to hide their identities and later these face-cut people or clans were given a name, *Amabhaca* (those who are hiding). Others called themselves *Amampondo* derived from the Ngoni word for horn, *Uphondo*.

Some people do have these "cuts" or "scars" on their skins that I'm talking about as we speak. That because many people entered into religion with these marks but most of all, with the *muthi* or *Izinsizi* in their blood systems.

In the past, elders used to believe in these kinds of sciences as much as they believed in the Divine Higher Power of their own understanding, *uMvelingqangi*. I often say that some Africans who follow Christianity don't even know what it is that is actually protecting them between Baal (who according to Isaiah and Lucifer is the Most High) and their forefathers. Some pastors or priests still possess in their blood the protection of *muthi* which was deepened in the skin by their great-grandfathers.

Here's another interesting story about *muthi*. It won't leave your body just because you go to church every Sunday. It remains with you until you die.

Hmm, let's see. I'm actually looking for a closer but relatable example we can use to make you understand this. Aha! I found one.

Look, as much as religion opposes tattoos. going to church every Sunday or every day for that matter will not erase them from your skin. They'll remain with you as part of your past, exactly like *muthi* from *Izingcabo* which can protect one until they die. It lingers in your blood system as a person lives. This then makes it difficult to understand which of the two, *muthi* and religion, is working more than the other or which one is more powerful.

What I know about our forefathers, especially from the little that I get from the stories of the past, is that they were not dull and stupid as the white man perceived them to be. I have learnt that they had great amounts of natural wisdom, survival skills and deep human intelligence attached to their lives and what they have paved for us as life. This seems to have ended when whites came to Africa. So, the kind of *muthi* or herbs they used are today used by white people in their customised but Western medicines.

So ,who's wise here?

It's easy to see but people still act as if they can't see anything! They're addicted to dressing all good and being ready to go to church every Sunday and everything and everyone else becomes water under the bridge.

But, I swear our forefathers wouldn't have even engaged with this Christian mediocracy if those who introduced it were not brutal and forceful towards them. It's no secret that they were brutally killed if they did not adhere to the ways of the Christian organisation. This is still a war maker in the Middle East because not every African or every nation in the world adhered to it. As a result, they were supposed to be dealt with and that is what caused some of those nations to be brutally murdered. Later, they formed a way to make it seem as if it was black on black violence.

How?

That is a good question. Look, if it wasn't for Christian leaderships such as Greece, Rome, US, UK, etc., Africa would have been a very peaceful continent. That's because even the guns and bombs used in these wars are distributed by the very Christian-influenced countries including the four mentioned above and that is no secret.

So, to cut a long story short, basically the message I'm trying to drive home here is that we need to remember who we are. If we do, we will start realising that we're lost. Because yes, we are lost!

And we need to be grounded to find peace within our family structures as Africans because the damage we're suffering is one which is cooked within families. It's manufactured and nurtured by us. Remember, we are the ones "responsible" for consuming what has been dividing us as families for years. *Phela*, it's no secret that we're so divided because of religion such as the likes of Christianity. This has been turned into some kind of tool used for isolation purposes or a device used for perpetrating a well-wrapped hatred, inequality, criticism, gossip, division and many more unfair behaviours and they're all practiced in secrecy by the so-called children of God.

Look, the aim is not to mirror back at Christians what they do to others but to remind them of the damage that they've caused by behaving in the manner that they do to other people who are not in alignment with Christianity. These would then be easily labelled as sinners.

But, it's no longer about who does what; it's about what and how we do then feel.

Perhaps the correct way is asking how do you feel or what it is that you feel, especially about yourself? Hmm. What do you feel? Despite everything you do and don't do and all that you pretend not doing while you do, what do you actually feel about yourself?

...*Cozi-coz' Yaphela!*

Kingship

Due to the influence of the Hebrews and the like, the Ngoni groups were learning slowly about what was happening in Egypt. They learnt about the leadership from the ex-slaves of Egypt who were then part of the AbaNgoni group.

Decades later after having to settle in the southern part of Africa, they officially grouped themselves into proper empires, transforming their clans into king-doms, to be precise.

Leadership structures such as cabinets were formed and slowly developed into traditional leadership. This included kings along with traditional healers, fortune tellers, generals and warriors. Senators and juries were elected and appointed amongst the existing but significant and relevant senior figures of each of those Ngoni-speaking groups. They were chosen according to their qualities and characteristics. Yes, it happened so.

These structures emerged across the Ngoni-speaking groups. For the first time, they had official leadership structures in place to ensure that the matters of their own communities were dealt with by the jury or the cabinet of the given kingdom.

This arrangement helped in reducing and dealing with conflicts that were troubling their groups' social, trade and commercial affairs and, of course, land matters.

This is where the matters of their people's livelihoods were discussed and kept among the leaderships structures before being advised or announced to the targeted memberships and the rank and file of the community/kingdom of these Ngoni-speaking people.

Remember, the emaSwati tribe, among all groups of the Ngoni-speaking people, were the first to have introduced a proper structure of Kingship (*ubuKhosi*). Hence, even the surname or the name, Nkosi was first heard from the emaSwati group amongst the Ngoni-speaking groups.

However, the formalisation of kingship structures was the best idea they've ever come up with. Besides, these were the descendants of the Handza people who were the most feared and oldest tribe.

So, their kingship structure became one which was reliable and it included quality figures. As you know, a king, like a president, needs to have a wall of warriors before him and his cabinet standing at his side. And should these senators and warriors be weak, the entire structure becomes vulnerable and could fall. But not the one of emaSwati. They maintained their kingdom over the years to this date.

After their first king was introduced, the conflicts which often led to wars amongst the Ngoni groups themselves stopped for a long time. Not only were these other groups learning from emaSwati's leadership and perhaps protecting their teaching and learning relations but they feared them too.

The number of people who joined the emaSwati group, especially after they've formed what seemed to others to have been a winning structure, rapidly increased the population. That's because people needed protection from invaders. They also needed assurance that the land they had migrated to and settled in different parts of Southern Africa was final and that they weren't going to be forced to relocate by wars.

However, there was pressure, frustration and fear among the groups that went further south and had already reached the coast. This included the likes of the AmaXhosa and those who later appeared as the Zulus or AmaZulu clan. According to the people of that time, they were said to have reached the end.

This then meant that the running was over. They then had to come up with a permanent plan. Some groups had already lost their pathfinders and strong men along the way, mainly due to malnutrition, wars, old age and illness.

The king of emaSwati was a trusted figure among all the groups of AbaNgoni people and that was before emaSwati reached present-day eSwatini. This was from the time of the first emaSwati king who was known as Hadzebe, derived from Hadzabe, a tribe found in Tanzania.

Later, he became known as *Inkosi*, hence the surname Nkosi, which was mothered by Hadzebe. He was a very significant figure in this group and was known for his leadership abilities and his ability to protect his people from enemies. That's what made a father, leader and later a king for these developed from the clans.

More than anything, they learnt about racism and the damage it caused to their groups which limited their potential to have an upper hand over other groups or enemies. However, the emaSwati stayed united and kept strong which later uplifted their flag unapologetically and fearlessly so.

This led to the king of emaSwati (who was the first *Inkosi* of the emaSwati Kingdom before the documented row of kings who followed after him who were allied to the British Empire) occupying a much larger portion of land than the other AbaNgoni groups.

Hence, the entire Mpumalanga Province, which is the largest province in the country, was the land of emaSwati or part of their kingdom. Even Pretoria, certain parts of Limpopo and a wider part of what is today known to be the Kwazulu Region (Kwa Mhlaba uyalingana and the likes) as opposed to the Kwazulu-Natal Region were also part of eSwatini. This means that half of South African once belonged to the emaSwati people. This is a true story. However, little do we know about how far the ruling and the power of the king of emaSwati reached.

Boy oh boy, it went as far as Mozambique. Certain parts of Mozambique are actually eSwatini. So, I hope you can see how far the emaSwati Kingdom had reached because despite their differences, they were a single tribe who possessed a remarkable leadership strategy that was never selfish and less brutal.

However, this never changed the fact that emaSwati themselves were a dangerous group amongst the entire Ngoni community.

What was it that made them so dangerous?

As I mentioned, their group was a combination of many different characters who all had their individual perspectives in beliefs. Later, they were ready and willing to be one and they then combined all their differences into a single belief system. This was their power and what actually resulted in them becoming emaSwati, the most feared group. But, I guess that's not enough. I still need to unpack this nicely so we're on the same page here. Right?

It is no secret that emaSwati were feared for their spirituality as they possessed the ability to perform spiritual warfare.

It was believed that their warriors were supernatural beings who could disappear into thin air while some could transform into certain creatures such as cats, birds, hyenas and wolves. But, that's not all. Some could transform and multiply into thousands of angry stinging bees. Some would temporarily turn into huge snakes and angry lions as some were believed to have undergone the process of *ukuthwala*where a spirit of an alien species would be forced to occupy the space of the individual's soul. This means that this very spirit would actually be in exchange for their soul for them to gain the spirit of the given creature of their individual choice.

That's what they believed in and at the time, it worked for them. Rather, should I say it actually worked for the era and for the next generations of emaSwati that followed. That's because even though some emaSwati clans were not in alignment with those kinds of tradi-tions, they all gained a reputation for being the most dangerous tribe. Besides; like I mentioned amongst them was an already feared group known as the Handza or Hadzabe people who are still known as the most dangerous tribe on Earth.

So that is a short explanation of why the emaSwati people were both feared and respected. However, that is not all. Amongst them were a group from

Egypt who were slightly different in nature and in understanding of what was then a new life to them (our forefathers). They possessed a great deal of knowledge known as "newer knowledge" as to how different things were done.

Some of them were slaves and sons and daughters of the slaves of ancient Egypt. Many of them possessed a set of skills shared to them by their own forefathers who taught them how to do different things. So, they kept their heads above water while living in the Kingdom of Egypt.

Some were known for their excellence in farming, some came from the families of craftsmen (who were known as Better Slaves back in Egypt; the type who could drink and smoke) and some were daughters and sons of war men, herbalists and healers. There were also traditional teachers who knew basic counting methods. Later, the group included traders who used to trade along the Nile River.

Some emaSwati clans would travel as far as the beaches of the Indian Ocean for trading purposes.

So, these were the things that made the emaSwati Kingdom highly decorated and believed to have had a strong structure amongst Ngoni people of the time.

emaSwati

But why emaSwati?

Look, if you're also out there asking yourself this very question then I guess you're right on time. Because this is the time when this question is about to be answered. I will answer it to the best of my ability which I still can't promise would be able to feed your appetite and curiosity but I'll sure give it a try.

We need to know that as languages change, a lot about us has changed as well. As our languages evolved, newer understandings were manufactured and the older ones faded into thin air within the midst of newer understandings of life. Time may have played a role but now it is us who are unravelling those changes.

Do you know why I say that?

We all know the truth but we all need to remember some of the things that will help us reach the finish line sane and alive. This life that we live may not necessarily be a race per se but it was built and arranged like one. The way you start in life is similar to the way runners begin their races too. They basically don't know how the race will end such as who will win, fall etc.

As much as each runner has trained and is going for the win, all of them know they may still lose the race. The funny thing is that none of them know what will cause them to lose.

Some will get dehydrated quicker than they may have anticipated which is likely to cause cramps along the race. Some would simply faint near the finish line. So, yes. Life is like that too.

We don't know what will make us or break us either. I've picked it up that our life journeys may be easily shortened or perhaps paralysed by the lack of knowledge of where we come from, of who we are and what we were about. We need to know what you and I are about or should be about. Yes, times have changed as many would claim. I agree times have changed but not for us to be fooled and then therefore be fools. We need to unpack our purposes in life within the system. We should not be divided and vulnerable. We should not become English-speaking emaSwati who don't even know what eSwatini looks like.

The lack of the knowledge of self is likely to lead us nowhere and very fast in our own individual life journeys, make that "purposes". At the end of the day, our lives should be formed by choices which are there to build our individual purposes. In other words, our lives are basically our purposes.

We will speak about purpose further, but for now we need to start by answering a question I left hanging at the beginning of this chapter. That is emaSwati. This is a very interesting name given it history and the rich story it carries.

So, I'll begin with the Ngoni word which refers to a newly developing branch or a stem of a tree, usually one which is greener and softer. It was used as some sort of whipping device when a child crossed the line.

I love how the tribe of emaSwati would use *uswazi*. They mainly used it as a form of defence during a battle. Okay, wait a minutes now. In what?

Lol. I guess the question you are asking yourself is why would anyone use a developing branch against angry warriors. I mean, who the hell in the seven earths does that? It's puzzling, isn't it?

But yes, that's what ancient emaSwati used during their battles where a couple of *izinswazi* (plural form of *uswazi*) would be carefully combined into one branch using certain grasses and wood bark. It would have a thick handle and a softer tip on the other end like a whip.

However, theirs would preferably be long to cause harm and discomfort to the opponent or enemy while they were a couple of feet away from the emaSwati warrior. I hope you picked up that I did mention that each whip of *uswati* could cause harm and discomfort to the skin of the victim. Yes, that's very true.

Remember, the emaSwati warriors were well-trained to fight using those weapons. Hence, even the manner in which those were used, the emaSwati warriors would have their own targets to hit and that would usually be the back. Ouch!

So that's why those had to be long enough to reach the person's back while they were two metres away from the source. And mind you, those weren't just sticks but they were well processed through *muthi* for it to cause irritations and then later, infections where one may have been hit. The wound would deepen and cause the flesh to open like you've been cut by a sharp blade.

This art of fighting was established by the ancestry of emaSwati, the Hadza people who lived their lives as a group of natives in the bushes along the Nile River. Hence, some of them are claimed to still exist in the Amazon Forest which somehow links to the Nile River.

Some are claimed to be in Tanzania while others joined the abaNgoni people who headed southward during migration up until eSwatini. However, there's something even more interesting about the use of *uswati* as a weapon.

This understanding has been adopted by another tribe of the AbaNgoni group, the Ndebele people. Here, the boys play a game of *uSwazi* (in isiNdebele and isiZulu language); because the one of *uSwati* belongs to the emaSwati people. However; the manner in which their *iziNswati* (soft sticks) were prepared by the emaSwati warriors appears to be similar to the manner in which amaNdebele boys would prepare theirs prior to their traditional game which is called *umdlalo wenswazi* in the Ndebele language.

The lining of the sticks and the tying method the Ndebele boys used resembles that of ancient emaSwati warriors' methods which were done to help strengthen and prolong the life of the sticks during the fights. They used certain animal fats to help soften the sticks but wait until you hear what the amaNdebele boys would normally use in replacement for what the emaSwati warriors would use for poisoning their *izinswazi* (soft sticks) which was *muthi*.

Lol! I laughed when I first heard this which from the horse's mouth. One of my old friends, Mpho, told me about it.

Mpho belong to the Masangu clan which is part of the amaNdebele group. He told me that they actually play this game after attending initiation school or *Ingoma.* During this game, the boys show off their strength and fighting skills of *Izinswazi* to the girls and elders of their villages.

The boys are required to fight with their shirts off (I guess that's where the showing of strength part comes in).

However, the sticks used during those games would have already been well marinated in a good mixture of animal fat, preferably that of a goat which has just been slaughtered. For some reason, I didn't get to hear properly because the conversation had to be slightly interrupted by the part where the chilli pepper gets to be added to the mixture.

Lol! I don't think I need to explain why they would do that. The combination says it all. Just picture a person's skin plus *uSwazi* plus chilli pepper. Do your own math here.

So, yes. That's what the boys of certain clans of amaN-debele would do to gain popularity amongst girls of their village. That must have been "chilli fun" to do or not to do.

But, that's not the point. The point here is the history behind the name emaSwati and what *uSwati* is in the context of abaNgoni language's explanation.

Before we get to the role that this beautiful tribe has played in liberating and fighting against what represented itself to be tribalism and oppression, we need to examine the 'virus' that kept on separating or dividing abaNgoni race into its present-day pieces.

Let's start with the era of King Shaka Zulu which was a huge threat to all the abaNgoni-speaking kingdoms. It was a ploy which was manufactured to ensure that the Zulu Kingdom expansion was devoured and it came from and was conducted by the emaSwati Kingdom.

They actually formed alliances with neighbouring Ngoni-speaking groups under the auspices of aiding liberation efforts among Ngoni-speaking people. This was in the form of displaying opposition towards what was a pipelined plan of the Zulu Kingdom which was expansion under the "whitish" and brutal rule of King Shaka Zulu.

Again, emaSwati gained an upper hand across all the Ngoni-speaking people. The Kingdom of eSwatini was once again trusted and believed in by many abaNgoni people and other kingdoms across Africa and other parts of the world such as Britain, who were dismally defeated by King Shaka's warriors during the battle of eSadlwana, known as *Impi Yase-Sandlwana*.

emaSwati warriors were feared and respected by even the Zulu warriors. So, this made the emaSwati Kingdom one which was greatly admired in the southern parts of Africa. eSwatini became the kingdom that other Nguni-speaking groups would go to for a warm shoulder to cry on whenever there was a crisis. One such example is when uMzilikazi (the founder of amaNdebele) was forced to flee KwaZulu to the region of Zimbabwe following conflicts in the Zulu Kingdom under King Shaka. He wanted to occupy the entire southern region up until Tanzania. He knew that this was where some of abaNgongi clans remained during their migration towards the south where they were found at the time. Hence, those were stories shared from one generation to the next.

It was King Shaka Zulu's desire to destroy all the empires and become king of the Ngoni people. Some clans had already given in to his ruling and their superiors had been brutally murdered and their people were taken into the Zulu Kingdom, thereby expanding King Shaka's kingdom. Not everyone was happy. Hence, uMzilikazi, who was the king's most powerful general (*Inceku yeNkosi*), decided to call it quits. This was after he had been having endless disputes over territorial and ideological differences with the king from 1819 to 1822. uMzilikazi then decided to take his family and leave in secrecy. However, some of the members of the Zulu Kingdom decided to rather stick with him. uMzilikazi was never an easy persona himself and he possessed a remarkable fighting spirit in him and some of the members of the kingdom knew that. They used to compare uMzilikazi's and Shaka's strength and in many cases, uMzilikazi would win the analytical vote of the rank and file of the empire. This led to uMzilikazi fleeing with approximately 400 to 500 followers including uLobhengula, one of Shaka's most trusted figures. uLobhengula taught Shaka Zulu how to fight the traditional stick fight.

uMzilikazi remained for at least two to three years while uSoshangane was gone. Later, in the fourth year, he followed in the footsteps of uSoshangane, another prominent general of King Shaka Zulu. It was believed that he fled during the Nyezana Battle.

This migration occurred in the years 1823 to 1826 when uSoshangane, one of the trusted but defected members of Shaka's army, migrated northward through eSwatini. He later established the Gaza Kingdom in present-day Mozambique. This gives us an inkling that they were a generation of the slaves of Egypt.

The word "Gaza" is derived from the Hebrew word *Azzah* which means strong or powerful. We get to hear about this word in the history of the Egyptians and Israelites in the far Middle East (in Africa). This is where the coastal region called the Gaza Strip (the border separating Egypt and Israel) is situated. The name of the largest city in the Gaza Strip is called Gaza City. In addition, Gaza was a district capital within the

Ottoman Empire and existed 300 years before the Gaza Kingdom of King uSoshangane. This was proven to have remained strong and powerful (as the Hebrew explanation of the word Gaza elaborates) for the Gaza Kingdom which is present-day Gaza Province still stands strong to this date.

It is important for emaSwati's generational pride and dignity generated from our rich history to know that for King uSoshangane and his followers to escape safely, the emaSwati Kingdom (our forefathers) played a huge role.

eSwatini was where they all had to pass through and be guided and sharpened on leadership skills before they continued on their journey. eSwatini became their cushion to fall back on, especially when they encountered territory politics or food supply issues in the name of refuging and sheltering them. This prevented issues they encountered from being resolved in deadly wars.

As you'd remember that it was the emaSwati warriors who stopped the Zulu warriors from chasing uMzilikazi and who were already proving to be his people at the Battle of uMhlathi-uze (present-day Mhlatuze River). This was where the emaSwati warriors once again proved the Zulu warriors wrong.

They managed to support uMzilikazi's group or what was slowly developing to be amaNdebele without any fear. They aided amaNdebele migrations and settlements unapologetically so. Shaka Zulu knew everything about that, but he was not going to be stupid and fight a battle he was going to lose anyway. Hence, he decided to back off.

That's what you need to know about yourselves. Mirroring who your forefathers were will assist you in shaking off the fear that Christianity has instilled in your brains which has made you fearful. It's been made part of your DNA because you've allowed it so by consuming the lies that Christian pastors or priests have made you know as life. Instead, it is the imitation of what could have been life, only if it was lived by the truth.

Look, we're good people. We've always been good people but we lack the knowledge that we're actually what we think or made to believe we are not. Until that knowledge fades, we shall not anticipate being who we truly are yet again but what the Bible tells us that we are and not.

History doesn't lie; people tell lies about it. We need to start embracing African writers to gain proper and meaningful mind visuals of what occurred in the distant past. Such knowledge can only be learnt from African storytellers through visions and dreams. Writers are not normal people. They see what others don't and they say what others won't simply because they can. That's not normal because according to the society in which each of us live, normal becomes what everyone else is doing or able to do. Isn't it so?

So, us writers usually don't think like normal people do. Our minds are complex, dynamic and creative entities with a remarkable sense of imagination as we constantly receive information from the Universal Signal or the Divine. It is a sense of observation as we are gifted with the art of noticing details. We see patterns and connections between seemingly unrelated things, people and places. We also possess a great sense of reflection as we get to analyse experiences, emotions, visions and thoughts to craft authentic reads for readers. We are gifted with the ability to see through things, people and places. It all relies on our patterns of thinking which are critical and unimaginable. Hence, we get to evaluate information, arguments and what "is" from perspectives. I guess that explains the kind of thinker that I am not.

Thanjekwayo Leading From Behind

Like I mentioned, history does not lie. This is especially true of the Thanjekwayos whose blood is truly thicker than water. Hence, in the history of emaSwati in general, the richer historical events of the entire emaSwati were preserved with the Thanjekwayos whose stories will forever be passed down through generations of the Thanjekwayo clan.

This is bigger than what the Thanjekwayos of this date know about themselves and where they come from.

Look, the reason why I had to briefly explain about the kingship is because we are one other generation of the royal bloodline within the spectrum of the sphere of the Kingdom of eSwatini. This means that if our history was well preserved and documented, there would be a king amongst the truer bloodline of the Thanjekwayos. One of you or your boy child would have been king.

However, the history of the existence of the Thanjekwayo clan faded with time. Before that, it started by falling into the hands of our enemy. It was somewhat exploited and fabricated and shoved into the wrong books.

But, not anymore. The truth will be brought forth. We deserve to know about ourselves; we need to understand who we are. And that can only be uncovered by a few.

Now, moving right on.

The rich history of the Thanjekwayos will astonish you (especially you, the Thanjekwayos' descendants) before you're even halfway through with this read. As I'm writing right now as we speak, more information is being sent to my brain by the Universal Signals in emphasising the Law of Attraction that I experience when my brain desires.

Okay, before I lose you. I think I'll have to begin where everything about this chapter should have started. That is to explain who Thanjekwayo was. I guess that should be the beginning point here. Hmm. What do you think?

You'll remember what I shared with you earlier about the Exodus which was a ground-shaker of a moment or era. It caused a great amount of expansion of the abaNgoni-speaking people who were then newly exposed to hearing different languages. Many of them were influenced by Hebrew and the Ngoni language but later these two languages created kiSwahili or Swahili language of the population from the North.

And now that I've mentioned that, which will still be linked with some information that we will later encounter in this very book:

Thanjekwayo was actually the son of King Ngwane or Sobhuza II and was born between 1785 and 1795. He and King Shaka Zulu were born around the same time. King Shaka was born between 1787 and 1795. His royal lineage proves that he is a descendant of the Khumalo clan. However, he remains a Dlamini or a Dlomo, a name of Sobhuza I. Thanjekwayo was a well-trained warrior like his father who became King Ngwane II. During his reign he was known to be either a Dlomo or Dlamini, whose forefathers originated from the community from as far as Ethiopia. They shared a bloodline with the Queen of Sheba also known as Bilqis. She was a biblical figure who admired King Solomon for his wisdom (Kings 10: 1-13). We see another link in the history of an Ethiopian figure, Hailey Selassie (1930-1974), who's also said to have possessed similar powers to those of Sobhuza I to III of the emaSwati Kingdom dating from the 17th century. This is like another but significant figure known as Sosobala who was also believed to have possessed this power. It was said that he could transform into a cat or thousands of bees if he liked. This was the kind of power that people from the far north were believed to possess. Hence, even the name "Ngwane" comes from a Hebrew word for colour or hue. It is known and pronounced as "Gwan" or "Guan". In the isiSwati language context, Gwane or Ngwane means "the conqueror" or "victor".

But then, what was the name of this significant figure, Thanjekwayo Dlamini, derived from?

Well, the name Thanjekwayo was a combination of two words — *Ethanjeni Kwayo* (right on its bone) which was quoted from the praises of his youth life (*izibongo zobunsizwa bakhe*). Thanjekwayo was good at stick fighting and the phrase *Ethanjeni-Kwayo* would refer to the kind of damage he could cause to an enemy's bones. It may have been used in this way: "*Wena Wendlunkulu; oshaya Ethanjeni Kwayo.*"

Izibongo would go on and on like a song or poem. As you'd recall that in the older times, abaNgoni young men would recite *Izibongo zensizw*a (praises of a young man). As much as they would also have praises to empower women or celebrate femininity known as*uKukhwezela* (to lay something over the other or empower or to add value). However, some were just praises to help preserve the cultural heritage of their clans, etc.

So, for that matter, each boy would be taught how to compose their own praises. This allowed them to talk about their backgrounds and the happenings of the era in which they lived. For a man would grow older with *Izibingo Zakhe* (his praises). Like the name of uSoshangane which developed after he was announced to have fled the Kwa-Zulu Kingdom. The truer meaning to it comes in two words, *uSoshiya-Ngane* (he who left his children behind), referring to his act of leaving his children behind (Kwa-Zulu) and fleeing.

However, it would differ with highly decorated figures such as Thanjekwayo whose praises would be sung at gatherings by the poet/s of the village. Like those of King Shaka Zulu known to be (*Izibongo Zika Shaka Zulu*).

"Wena we Zulu… Ilembhe eleqa amanye amalembe ngokukhalipha…uShaka akashayeki…"

These are what formulated *izibongo zensizwa* like it did with Shaka. However, even then the poet would still need to consult with the given royal figure such as King Shaka. It was best for the poet to first consult with King Shaka before proceeding to dig their own grave with their tongue. Lol! I bet Shaka would cut off that thing, if not do what he did best and spear the hell out of whoever spoke ill of him and his leadership. So, yes. That's what the praises were about.

And then later, during the era of "names" or "naming" which promoted a policy that each of them should then consist of "one name" which was accompanied by "one surname". This never existed in Africa for thousands of years until white people came and changed everything. That's why our forefathers, despite those new naming methods, continued and added what we present-day know to be a clan name (*izibingo or izithakazelos*). These were to play the part of *Izibongo Zabo* which, according to white people, no longer existed.

However, even then, many of those "one names" were quoted from existing praises that many men already owned. This was the reason why *izibongo,* present-day "surnames", were attached to men rather than women. For it was men who owned *izibongo* (praises).

But for those who never had any; they would rather make up their own names which were also not random but relevant to who or what they believed they were. For example, like the Nhlengethwa clan (the dolphin). This represented the kind of wisdom this clan carried as it is believed to this date that dolphins are the humans of the sea.

Then, you have your Ndlovu clan (the elephant). Their name had to do with their body appearance and their weight. Hence to this date, many people who possess the Ndlovu surname appear with a much thicker bone structure. The list goes on and you find surnames such as Dlamini and the likes of Ndlangamandla, which their origin directly duplicated and emphasised on who they truly were in nature.

Okay, we'll start with Dlamini and the meaning behind it. But before I do that, I'd like to highlight that this is not to actually speak ill of the Dlamini clan founders. However, it is true that in ancient times, Africans were proud traditional *muthi* users. Even those who'd do it for bad purposes were proud to say it in their raises that "they were murderers". But, you still need to understand the language used by aBalayi, present-day aBaloyi. to understand what these names and certain phrases they used meant.

For instance, *ukudla* (also known as eating) was a word transformed from its original meaning and used as a "coding word" for "traditionally murdering someone" using *muthi* or magical or scientific practices. Hence, this clan were proud to call themselves "day-murders" which in the aBaloyi language it would literally mean (*aBadla-emini*). Like oNdlanga-mandla who were known for regularly committing bad deeds. Hence, *Dlangamandla* meaning, "eating/murdering violently or at a high pace". These names had attached to them direct meanings as opposed to a couple of them which were developed in style, like the name Malinga by our forefathers.

This makes sense when you read it backwards like Ngalima. This could have been one of many names which were used wisely in hiding some background (don't you think?).

And, speaking of Malinga. Many members of this family need to find out how the Malinga clan combine with Thanjekwayo. Okay, I'll begin with the Malinga clan. There is no conclusive evidence that the Malinga surname may have originated in Egypt. However, consider that when the Exodus occurred, it was long before the "surname" policy was introduced.

So, it was like many names of the African diaspora which might have developed from migrations as cultures blended along their travels which led them to the South.

This is where some of the existing names developed from, like the Malinga name. This may have explained the role that this figure may have played back in the Egyptian empire or perhaps I should use the word "exile", serving as one in a community of Better Slaves.

The role that Malinga as an entity or figure played back in ancient Egypt had a lot to do with art and culture. This involved agriculture (hence Ngalima), animal husbandry, singing and he was also a good warrior. This made him a great asset back in Egypt as it is in present-day eSwatini Kingdom.

However, history seems to have repeated itself because even within the eSwatini Kingdom, the Malinga clan has always been known for holding prominent positions within the eSwatini Kingdom. This includes being advisors, warriors and nobles of the king.

The king who actually was the founder of the eSwatini Kingdom was King Ngwane II. He was the father of this notable figure in the entire history of emaSwati, uThanjekwayo.

uThanjekwayo was the one who led the emaSwati nation to their destination, present-day eSwatini Kingdom, where they've settled and were never allowed to be shaken. He did everything in the name of protecting his father's legacy of kingship which at the time made him the prince.

Time went by and his father, King Ngwane II, was poisoned in the midst of the first battle between emaSwati and other Nguni-speaking groups (*Imfecane*) who wanted expansion of what was later known to be called the Zulu clan which was founded by Shaka Zulu himself.

1815

The Genesis Of Infecane

The battle when King Ngwane II died (1815) was not conducted by King Shaka Zulu. Both he and Thanjekwayo were almost the same age then and may have been involved in the battle but the fight was never led by Shaka Zulu. Also, King Ngwane II was not killed on the battlefield. By then, he was already sick and old to be on the battlefield. Yes, it was the era of the battles for kingdom expansions but he was not killed in battle. King Ngwane II was poisoned by an unknown rival clan member in the name of white sabotage.

Slowly, the dirty and hairy hands of the white man got closer and closer. But, it was still unknown to the majority because they were still unseen but heard of. The person to questionably temporarily hold King Ngwane's II throne was his wife, Queen Ndvungunye, until the next king was officially announced.

But, there seemed to be great conflict as Queen Ndvungunye was a younger wife amongst the wives of King Ngwane II. She wanted her son to become the successor of his father's throne and that caused great disputes in the royal family.

Even the rank and file knew who was the rightful successor and that was Thanjekwayo. He actually didn't want to become king however, his mother, Queen Ntombi Ndwandwe (the daughter of King Zwide's brother), insisted that he do. However, she wouldn't have won that complex polygamy battle by herself because her son wasn't even part of the argument. He was still curious to find out who might have been responsible for his father's death. Queen Ntombi belonged to the Ndwandwe Kingdom and the Ndwandwes maintained good relations with King Ngwane II, precisely with the Kingdom of eSwatini. They also knew about the late King Ngwane's vision and desire about who was to become the successor to his throne and not when he was already dead.

This had a lot to do with having his son, Thanjekwayo, enthroned as king while he was still alive. This might have been the reason for his death. Someone didn't want Thanjekwayo to become king of emaSwati. A couple of months later, the matter was resolved and this started the *Infecane* movement. The jury was fair and conducted the matter as the late king may have anticipated and the son of his own choice was traditionally enthroned as king.

From then onwards, the emaSwati Kingdom gained more popularity. Thanjekwayo was favoured by the masses and famous before he became king. This proved that he was not only his father's choice but that of the people as well, not to mention the Ndwandwe Kingdom. Thanjekwayo enhanced Swati/Ndwandwe relations (which was never permanent) after his mother had tried to make peace between the two kingdoms for many years. She also navigated the complex family dynamics, including King Ngwane's multiple wives, especially after the king had passed on. The politics within the royal family kept on piling but the queen was a wise, diplomatic and strong figure. She ensured that Thanjekwayo was guided on how to rule and rule genuinely.

Hence, Thanjekwayo became a profound and charismatic leader who uplifted the spirit and the wishes of his mother and helped shape emaSwati culture and traditions. And given the fact that his father was actually the founder of emaSwati and him having to play a crucial role in doing so, it made it easy for his followers to adhere to what he had to say. This gave him a good platform to unify the emaSwati group and strengthen the kingdom.

Like King Shaka, King Thanjekwayo conducted his own military campaigns to expand the emaSwati kingdom. He was a true warrior and fought King Shaka on the battlefield a few times during the battles for expansion. There were also conflicts about cattle which resulted in battles but this is when they were both still younger and not kings. Both the emaSwati clan and the amaZulu clan knew these two as their upcoming kings, despite all the politics and rumours which were known to be likely to not make them kings. However, they were still the choice of the people of their kingdoms.

As much as emaSwati may have wanted a king who was even wiser, they also needed a king who could protect them. Thanjekwayo Dlamini had already proven to have done that before he became king. The same applies to Shaka Zulu who at the time was also one of the trusted and feared kings because of his natural wisdom and violent tendencies.

These were the kinds of figures who were so unpredictable, you wouldn't have known and be sure of what was going to happen next. However, on the other hand, Shaka was already showing signs of brutality

which still didn't change that he still was a very strategic young man. Of course, he also had his mother
backing him to become king despite any known
circumstances which could stop him from becoming
king of the Zulu Kingdom.

His biggest threat was that he was "colonising" all
the amaNgoni-speaking groups and turning them
into one clan, the Zulus. This information reached the
emaSwati Kingdom and they knew about his plans.

Remember, not every clan wanted to become Zulu.
Some refused but given the brutality of King Shaka,
none of them would come out and say it out loud.
Shaka would kill anyone whose intentions had connotations of working against his authority and that was
no secret.

So, they needed a better kingdom to turn to. Like, I
mentioned, the emaSwati Kingdom was one which
was always open and ready to offer assistance to other
abaNgoni groups.

I want you to make up your own mind and I am not,
in any manner, trying to accuse King Shaka of being
responsible for his father's death, uSenzangakhona
ka Jama (he was the son of King Jama Dlamini). This
then makes Shaka ka Senzangakhona a Dlamini as
opposed to a Zulu. But, it can still be argued that
when he was born, he became Senzangakhona ka
Thethwa, a very tricky name. But, I want you to make
up your own mind.

This was 1815 (please mark that), the year when the king of emaSwati, King Ngwane II, the father of Thanjekwayo, died. Shaka, who was no king at the time, promised that once he became king, no other kingdom would exist as he would destroy each and every one of them. You can imagine that must have been every empire's greatest threat.

Remember, Shaka's mother, Nandi, the daughter of a historical figure called Bhebhe, had to go into exile with Shaka. She fled to the Mthethwa clan where Shaka gained military experience. He then returned to his father's kingdom (which was then the Dlamini kingdom of Jama, the father of Senzangakhona).

King Jama Dlamini was the cousin-brother of King Ngwane II or Sobhuza Dlamini II. By then, Shaka was no longer the boy they used to know but a beast.

So, even though Senzangakhona may have been no real father to Shaka as it was widely suspected across the kingdom led by Senzangakhona, he who was supposed to be his father and to many clans of the abaNgoni groups, especially those who had close relations with the emaSwati Kingdom.

1816

The Game Changer

Remember, the previous year, 1815, the king of emaSwati died and Shaka started his military campaign to expand the Zulu nation. This was the era of fear amongst the abaNgoni clans and kingdoms. However, it was puzzling to the emaSwati Kingdom as to why would Thanjekwayo, whose had just been announced king early that very year, began hearing rumours that Shaka (who was Thanjekwayo's cousin) was embarking on a military campaign that was similar to his. That was a puzzling one.

That because that was a campaign that was master-minded by Thanjekwayo in secrecy against the Kingdom of Jama, present-day Kwa-Zulu. This followed the poisoning of his father which Thanjekwayo suspected was manufactured and orchestrated by the Ndwandwe clan who were trying to speed up the process of him (Thanjekwayo) becoming king of emaSwati. This was before Shaka was announced king. And you'll find out why they did that.

The Ndwandwe clan knew that Shaka was being readied for kingship and trained to be a leader by the Mthethwa clan. They also wanted to speed up the process of Shaka becoming king of what was going to be AmaZulu.

So, it was in the courtesy of helping Thanjekwayo when they produced a poisonous potion which murdered the king of emaSwati, King Ngwane II, the father of Thanjekwayo. Remember, the Ndwandwe clan had full access to the emaSwati Kingdom via their daughter, Queen Ntombi, the mother to Thanjekwayo, who was married to the king of emaSwati.

This then made it easy for them to overthrow King Ngwane II on behalf of Thanjekwayo (who didn't even about the plan at the time). In 1816, he was pronounced king and took a name that resembled his father's, Sobhuza. He was announced as Thanjekwayo Sobhuza Dlamini, also known as Sobhuza III.

But, wait until you hear what was happening in the Kingdom of Jama in the process.

Well, exactly when Thanjekwayo was pronounced king, it was the very same era when Shaka's father was pronounced dead. He was also poisoned. The number one suspect was Shaka but he pointed the blame at Mfolozi, his uncle, who was Senzangakhona's brother. He also desired to become king. A week after his father's royal burial, Shaka was announced as king.

The rise of Shaka was indeed stimulated by his father's death. And because he had proven on multiple occasions that he would become king, no one opposed it. Shaka was announced king in the very same year that Thanjekwayo was also enthroned as king of emaSwati.

Shaka was brutally abused by the Dlamini clan forcing his mother, Nandi Ka Bhebhe Langeni, to flee with him. As such, he didn't want anything to do with the Dlamini name. While he was in exile, he was made to discard Senzangakhona as his father.

It shows that indeed the Mthethwa clan was somewhat paving their way inside the Kingdom of Jama as they knew it would be in Shaka's hands. By then Shaka was like a son to the king, Dingiswayo, his mentor. This meant that should he become king, they knew it would assist them to gain access, if not influence, in the Zulu Kingdom from the 'shades'.

The news that Shaka was king did not sit well with Thanjekwayo; who already knew that Shaka had stolen his military campaign plan to expand the emaSwati Kingdom which his father would have loved.

Besides, who was then King Shaka and not Dlamini but Zulu precisely? King Shaka Zulu had already sent *Izigijimi* (messengers) to spread his word that he was now king and that he was going to come for each and every kingdom that existed.

So, King Thanjekwayo was fuming in anger and he also sent his own messengers known as *eMasosha Embango* to go around his kingdom and gather men to be warriors from each clan that existed in present-day eSwatini Kingdom.

Two years later, King Thanjekwayo had gathered a troop of more than 1,800 warriors. Surprisingly, many of those men came from outside Swaziland and they belonged to many different clans of the Ngoni-speaking groups, especially those who were also against the brutal rule of King Shaka Zulu. He was a real threat because he was king and his word was final. These warriors would encounter Shaka when they fought with the Mthethwa clan where Shaka Zulu was somehow used as a weapon in return for his stay. But, the young man enjoyed himself with other young men on the ground during the ancient but secret operations of stealing cattle from other clans.

This was said to have been changed by Shaka during his youth times when other boys feared that he would beat them and take their cattle to the Mthethwa clan. This young man was bad news when it came to wrestling and stick fighting. When he grew up, he was a combination of both a wrestler and a stick fighter. These incidences were countable because King Thanjekwayo was hearing about them from different men who belonged to widely separated clans but who were then part of the emaSwati warriors in return for their stay in the kingdom. King Thanjekwayo was no stranger to such news. He also fought against Shaka and won. So, he knew that the time was coming when Shaka would seek vengeance but in a different manner. Thanjekwayo was a king but Shaka wanted to take the crown away from him. Not only that but Shaka also wanted to take away his land and his dignity after losing to Thanjekwayo a few years earlier.

Mind you, Shaka had already proven to be a bully amongst his peers and he had gained the upper hand. However, all that changed when he was faced by yet another greater young man of his size whose remarkable stick fighting skills were known across the emaSwati clan.

This is what made the emaSwati Kingdom the go-to territory in times of war. It was due to the calibre of man that Thanjekwayo was. He was one of the strongest kings of the time and that is why King Shaka Zulu targeted the emaSwati Kingdom. It was the most high-profile kingdom in terms of structure. So, this made many men from the abaNgoni clans of the Ngoni-speaking groups want to become emaSwati and be protected from Shaka's brutal attacks.

They trusted King Thanjekwayo. He was a strategic planner of warfare, his military experience was greater than that of King Shaka and they knew it. Probably Shaka knew it too.

But, of course, not even he could do it by himself. He needed those men. Some even wanted citizenship within the eSwatini Kingdom. They came with their families and cattle to seek permanent settlements in return for being warriors or war men.

And indeed, many clans got access to portions of land to farm and live on. Even then, King Thanjekwayo was strategic about this. He located all the strong war men and traditional doctors near and around the border lines, trying to occupy as much land as possible.

That's where the Malinga clan began adding more value to the emaSwati Kingdom. Mind you, there's always been a deep bio-connection that links the Dlamini and the Malinga clans. Thanjekwayo who was a Dlamini from the time his father was alive. He always relied on the Malinga clan for wisdom and winning military strategies. The Malinga clan was rich with farmers and warriors. They possessed a great leadership structure in their doings and they were a "no nonsense" group amongst the Ngoni-speaking groups who chose peace instead.

The king needed them for their ability to plan. They were a small but very strong clan in terms of belief structures. Many in this clan were art lovers; they loved singing and dancing. They worked with every king of the emaSwati Kingdom, from King Sobhuza Nkosi I, the Brother of Sobhuza II, who went by the name Dlamini as opposed to Nkosi.

The value that the Malinga clan members added to the emaSwati leadership led to many of them holding prominent positions within the eSwatini Kingdom. This proves a deep royal connection. They were the advisors to the king and they were trusted because they were an extended family within the family tree of the Nkosis and the Dlaminis.

Well, let's break this down.

The Malinga clan is part of the Khumalo clan and this was also Thanjekwayo's royal lineage. He was a *Dlamini-Nkosi wesidlubula dledle saka Lobambha, siyabadla siyaba dlukulisa.* This also somehow explains the era they belonged to and it also carried meaningful genealogical ties with the king of that era.

This was to trace the lineage and the ties which then came with an art of revealing the shared ancestry and the clan affiliation. For example, the Malingas and the Dlaminis or Nkosis descend from King Ngwane II. Then, the Khumalos or abe-Khubalo descend from

King Ngwane I. This then makes the Khumalo, Malinga and Dlamini clans part of the royal family or the Kingdom of emaSwati.

This was one of many reasons why King Ngwane III or Thanjekwayo would deploy his army and himself to the battle of Mhlatuze River during the escape of the Ngoni group which was later labelled amaNdebele. They were led by who was later King

Mzilikazi who was a cousin of both King Shaka and Sobhuza III or Thanjekwayo, the notable figure who fought for the rights of the abaNgoni groups in general.

His great power was to fight for all that was right. In most of his battles, he made it a mandate that no troop should leave camp without being accompanied by the presence of the Malinga warriors.

Again, you should be able to pick up the importance of the Malinga clan members. They were part of the king's military plans, hence it is no secret that Thanjekwayo maintained an alliance with the Malinga clan leaders during military campaigns.

According to my own but general knowledge, no king will form a military alliance and take most of his advice from those they do not trust. This then proves the deep loyalty that the Malinga clan leaders shared with the Kingdom of emaSwati.

The close relations that King Thanjekwayo shared with the Malinga clan seemed mutual and genuine. Many were puzzled about whether or not Thanjekwayo possessed the Malinga surname.

He often visited the place where senior Malinga clan members dwelt. This place was called Kugege. It was a secret place that was of great importance to the king.

This adds to what is said about King Thanjekwayo being a very wise and tricky persona of note.

Mind you, it was through the input of Thanjekwayo that the cultural heritage of emaSwati was preserved. He even went the extra mile and established a set of what are present-day essential emaSwati traditions and customs. This includes *uKuteka* as opposed to *uKulobola*. He twisted a few things around.

So instead of calling the place Kwa-Gogo or Ku-Gogo, he used the name Ku-Gege. It was hidden to protect senior members of the Malinga clan from their rivals. However, the name has a deeper meaning to it, which was to refer to ku-Gogo. The same applies to places such as Kwa-Hhohho. This was to refer to Kwa-Gogo but the era of wars wouldn't allow certain people, places and things to be called by their original names and words which were familiar to the Ngoni-speaking groups.

Here is another thing you need to know about Thanjekwayo.

As I mentioned, he twisted things around. To this date, Kugege is still known as Kwa-Thanjekwayo, the place where Thanjekwayo himself referred to as Kwa Gogo.

That's because not only the Malingas stayed there but also his grandmother, Gogo Mavuso. He didn't want to put his grandmother at risk, hence he named the place Ku-Gege as opposed to its original meaning, Ku-Gogo. He ensured his grandmother's safety by surrounding her with Malinga warriors. They were also used to secure the kingdom's borders along with the Dlomos who are also part of the Dlamini clan.

Thanjekwayo was more than a king; he became a teacher. He passed on his wisdom and method of kingship to the next generation of the kings of emaSwati that followed after him.

Wars

As you'd recall that while King Thanjekwayo was getting prepared for what smelt like war, King Shaka, on the other end, was also getting himself prepared.

By late 1816, King Thanjekwayo was already long prepared and somehow got tired of waiting and checking over his shoulders for Shaka. He decided to gather a group of at least 20 well-trained men and head southward to the Zulu Kingdom. By right, this was his uncle's empire before he died. Shaka then assumed power and turned it into the Zulu clan. This made King Shaka Zulu his cousin.

Even though King Thanjekwayo didn't have much fear for King Shaka, his aim was to play a negotiator and mediator of some sort. He wanted to stabilise the situation while trying to ease the tension among all the Ngoni-speaking groups. King Thanjekwayo's eye could see beyond what was developing to be "white manipulation". In secret, he was already speaking of the divide they were already causing. Though he may have never been able to figure it out, he still had a great sense that they were not good people and that the Ngoni kingdoms and clans needed to be protected from whites.

He opened a discussion about that with King Shaka on a very special historical day.

However, King Shaka was a very shady person. He surprisingly welcomed them as per royal tradition where an ox was slaughtered for the royal visitors to feast on. The day was treated as normal and he listened to what the king of emaSwati had to say. After the meeting, the moment was well celebrated and the meat and traditional beer were dished out amongst the emaSwati warriors. But still, he wasn't clear about what needed to happen next. He randomly skipped the part where he was expected to comment about white people.

Midnight

During the midnight hour, King Thanjekwayo's uncle, Senzangakhona (King Shaka's father), appeared to him in a dream. He commanded him to leave immediately. He woke up and did as he was instructed. Half of his men were still awake and he told them to leave the Zulu Kingdom immediately. The men wouldn't have argued with the king even though they may had concerns about leaving at night. They started packing their belongings in silence and were "magically" off.

They left.

The next morning, they were nowhere to be seen. Their escape was untraceable. That's when King Shaka Zulu began having suspicions about their visit.

Again, King Thanjekwayo's visit to him became that which would turn dangerous and deadly because he didn't really have a clear understanding of the true motive behind it. And Shaka didn't want anything to bypass him. He wanted to be ahead and above everything around him. And when he couldn't, he got angry.

By now, you should know what was likely to happen when he got angry. "*Yimihlolo ke le!*" he explained. From then on his name changed from Thanjekwayo or Sobhuza to uSomhlolo.

Bloody 1817

You'd recall that King Ngwane II married the princess of the Ndwandwe clan. She became Queen Ntombi Ndwandwe, the mother to King Thanjekwayo. His name was then changed by the Zulus and many other Ngoni-speaking clans who already knew him as Somhlolo.

So, King Shaka used that to his own advantage to get King Thanjekwayo's attention. He deployed all his troops to the Ndwandwe Kingdom and made it look like a war that was related to border wars and expansion. His troops were told to destroy everything that moved within the Ndwandwe Kingdom. This led to widespread migration. The war lasted for at least three years until the Ndwandwe Kingdom was demolished and burnt to ashes (but wait and hear how). Many people died, especially from the Ndwandwe clan, starting with the army and many people within the kingdom. The survivors were left with no choice but to become part of the emaSwati Kingdom while a few surrendered to the Zulu clan and joined them. Mind you, the Zulu Kingdom was slowly losing members, including uMzilikazi who was then still King Shaka's general. He questioned the Ndwandwe attacks that the king was planning. He tried to resolve the matter through dialogue but King Shaka was not much of a negotiator. It was his way or no way at all. The biggest argument started when Mzilikazi suggested that Shaka did what Thanjekwayo came to his kingdom for and had recently did by even bringing a few of his war men when he came and visited Shaka for a few talks.

As you'd recall, that incident when Thanjekwayo and his warriors disappeared without a trace was still on the top of Shaka's mind. To him that was a threat; it really did shake his tree. So, when Mzilikazi made comments about Thanjekwayo, he literally poured petrol on an existing fire.

Shaka didn't want to hear anything about Thanjekwayo during those days. However, instead of heading to the emaSwati Kingdom, he decided to go to the Ndwandwe king.

The first encounter which was in a form of an ambush by Shaka was took place at midnight. Zwide's warriors were not expecting anything like that, especially from the Zulu Kingdom. According to them, it could have been the Mthethwa Kingdom with whom they had clashed a few months earlier before Shaka became king.

Shaka's battle was expected to be against the emaSwati Kingdom. This was especially after the rumours which mushroomed across all kingdoms that Thanjekwayo had visited King Shaka's kingdom and magically left without saying his formal goodbyes.

So, given that scenario, many thought it was going to be the emaSwati Kingdom which was going to be in trouble.

At first, Mzilikazi was forced to be part of the attack against the Ndwandwes. The poor guy was the general for goodness' sake and he knew that King Shaka would kill him if he didn't obey his orders. He didn't want to be seen as disobeying King Shaka's authority which could be deadly anyway.

However, he was never happy about that entire operation and how it was conducted. He found it unnecessary and unreasonable. That's because both the kingdoms of Shaka's father, Senzangakhona, and that of the Ndwandwe clan had always existed on the same ground. Even though there were conflicts, they had learnt to resolve them through talks and did not engage in any serious battles. That continued for ages until the honourable Shaka Zulu became king.

Look, Mzilikazi was a reasonable man. He was trying to be smart or should I say make Shaka Zulu think smarter as well. He was always using facts rather than fiction to navigate thoughts. Not only did he want Shaka to think smarter but he was also reasonable to the Ndwandwe clan because deep down, he knew that the motive that drove Shaka had less to do with the Ndwandwe clan or kingdom expansion as it is called in history written by the white man. Indirectly, he was provoking Thanjekwayo. However, eventually the battle was going to, one way or the other, increase the number of his followers or the population of amaZulu. Besides, Mzilikazi had earned respect from the Ndwandwe clan for consolidating and stabilising the tense situation between the Zulu and Ndwandwe kingdoms. So, in trying to advise Shaka not to go to the Ndwandwe clan in the form of an ambush was a way to distance himself from Shaka's operation and not look stupid to the Ndwandwe Kingdom.

Mzilikazi wasn't a fool. He sure was able to identify the hidden reason for Thanjekwayo's visit. He knew that Thanjekwayo might have gotten the message that Shaka's messenger once delivered to the emaS-wati Kingdom. That message was that once Shaka was king, he would destroy every kingdom that ever existed, including emaSwati.

When Thanjekwayo visited Shaka, he never mentioned a word about that message. King Shaka didn't mention it either. On the day of that weird and random visit by Thanjekwayo, even the rank and file of the Kingdom of the Zulus including Shaka's warriors were surprised at how Shaka treated him. A few days before that King Shaka was ready to destroy the emaSwati Kingdom and kill the king of emaSwati. Yet, an ox was even slaughtered in honour of Thanjekwayo and his men. It turned out to be a normal and civil conversation with laughs and jokes being shared among the kings. That was so surprising and confusing to them at the same time. They expected to see Shaka slaughtering Thanjekwayo as opposed to an ox, especially after he had brought himself to his "hunter".

The act of Shaka Zulu on the day left everyone surprised. More than that, it said a lot about the man Shaka Zulu claimed he was.

Well, I hate being the one saying it but do you think Shaka Zulu was hiding his great fear for King Thanjekwayo when he pretended that he liked him and acted more civil than expected? Because it smells like it...

So, uMzilikazi could tell that Shaka wanted to prove that he was still powerful and that he could still be dangerous to the "innocents" by attacking the Ndwandwe clan. He knew about Shaka's fear which made him angry and he didn't want to play a part in Shaka's power-hungry anger manifestation.

To be honest, Shaka was power hungry and he felt he had lost when Thanjekwayo came to visit his kingdom (especially after he had sent a messenger to advise him about his recent enthronement and that he was going to destroy the emaSwati Kingdom). That must have been very confusing indeed to those who didn't know the truth, but not to uMzilikazi who could see right through Shaka. He could easily see that his acts had connotations of fearful behaviours.

So, during the first ambush of the Ndwandwe clan (known as the Battle of Gqoki Hill), the general had to be there despite his disagreements with the king. At the end of the day, Shaka's word was final. He was king, remember. Despite the hour of the day when it took place, the first ambush was never really a success. The Ndwandwe Kingdom was filled with experienced warriors who wouldn't go down without a fight.

This then led to the following year's battle of 1818.

In that year's battle, the Zulu Kingdom had made allies with other Ngoni-speaking kingdoms such as the Mthethwa Kingdom led by King Dingiswayo and the Qwabe Kingdom led by King Phakathwayo.

You will recall that the Qwabe Kingdom was a very strong kingdom at the time, especially during the reign of Shaka's father, King Senzangakhona.

The Qwabe Kingdom was put on the map by King Langa, Senzangakhona's father. It kept on thriving over the years until the reign of King Shaka Zulu. Prior to Shaka's enthronement, especially when he was so desperate to become king, he lingered between the Qwabe and the Mthethwa kingdoms, going back and forth seeking help and knowledge.

This was where Shaka became knowledgeable about the art of kingship. He had a secret interest in the Mthwthwas and wanted to use their bloodline to become king of the Zulus, which he eventually became. However, you'll also get to hear what else one of these families may have introduced Shaka to in return for the abnormal powers he was known to possess.

But, what made Shaka turn his attention from General uMzilikazi and desiree to form alliances with these two kingdoms? Besides, uMzilikazi was sceptical and Shaka saw him as a great threat because he had proven many times before that he didn't fear him personally but he respected him as king. uMzilikazi was a true warrior and a good strategist as well.

During the second attack on the Ndwandwe Kingdom, uMzilikazi did not join the troops on the battlefield. He basically did not want to partake in those operations and he wasn't the only one. He did assist here and there in the campaign, however, his reluctance to go to the battlefield resulted in Shaka no longer trusting him. Subsequently, he went to the Mthethwa and the Qwabe kingdoms to request help. But why?

Why would Shaka need the help of those two kingdoms, especially if his kingdom was said to be strong with great warriors and all that? Also, Mzilikazi's lack of interest would not have been something that should have pushed him that far to ask for help from Qwabe and the like clans. This is especially true if he still trusted his army and his art of war. It becomes questionable, doesn't it? It's basically doesn't make military campaign sense.

Well, let me help you. The king had a great fear that the Kingdom of emaSwati might be present in the Mhlathuze River during their battle with the Ndwandwe clan. But, wait until you hear what happened.

Well, what King Shaka suspected might have been true but no, King Thanjekwayo may have been a very simple man but not so obvious. Yes, both the Ngwane and the Ndwandwe kingdoms were obviously known for being allies, especially in times of war, but not this time.

At the time, the emaSwati Kingdom led by King Thanjekwayo was obviously expected to engage in the Battle of uMhlathuze in support for the Ndwandwe clan. However, King Zwide had made an agreement with the Ngwane/emaSwati Kingdom that even if he loses the battle, his people must migrate to present-day eSwatini rather than being taken by force into the Zulu Kingdom. For that reason, King Zwide asked King Thanjekwayo of the emaSwati Kingdom to not get directly involved in the uMhlathuze River Battle. He told him to spare himself for the responsibility of refuging the Ndwandwe clan, some of which (especially the elderly) had already migrated to eSwatini.

But, another great movement was slowly unfolding as the elderly migrated from the Ndwandwe to the emaSwati Kingdom. King Thanjekwayo was having secret meetings with uSoshangane and the agenda had focused a lot on the amaZulu military campaign against the Ndwandwes. uSoshangane would leak some of the information about the campaign of the Battle of Mhlathuze to King Thanjekwayo who would then later share it with the Ndwandwe clan.

Mind you, the planning for this war took about a year.

uSoshangane wasn't the only one playing a part in that deadly agenda. King Shaka's general, uMzilikazi, the son of Mashobane, was also involved. Both he and uSoshangane shared the same values and interests of protecting and preserving their reputations. They didn't want their names to perish together with that of Shaka. Instead, they wanted to separate themselves from what was already panning out to be the brutal ruling of King Shaka. They both possessed great support from the rank and file of the Kingdom of Kwa-Zulu. That's because some of them were not in alignment with the ruling of King Shaka which caused great fear amongst them as they were the people who actually made up the population of the empire. This is just like the present-day ANC which doesn't care much about its own voters but the votes. Something like that.

uMzilikazi's secret agenda with the King of emaSwati, King Thanjekwayo, was to actually make sure that while King Shaka was away he too, along with his allies, was planning for the war.

uSoshangane would also head northward to present-day Eswatini where he would meet with the King of emaSwati.

It was during this time when the arrangement of both uSoshangane and uMzilikazi made them gain trust in the Kingdom of emaSwati and would later go through eSwatini during their migrations when they escaped from Kwa-Zulu. They formed ties with the emaSwati Kingdom and their plan seemed to have worked wonders.

Here's another untold story you may want to hear about. As you'd remember what I said about uSoshangane who was trusted by King Shaka in terms of war strategy. uSoshangane also possessed the spirit of a hunter or pathfinder and above all, he fought well. Hence, uMzilikazi ordered him to train some of the members of the emaSwati army on how to fight against King Shaka's warriors during the uMhlathuze River Battle. By then Shaka's army was ready known for their "horn attack" strategy.

Besides, uSoshangane knew Shaka when they were very young. He would teach him a skill or two when they grew up because uSoshangane was older than King Shaka. Besides, King Shaka grew up a very weak boy even compared to his peers.

So, despite Shaka's escape into exile which made him grow up under the Mthethwa clan, uSoshangane knew Shaka and his weaknesses. So, because the king of the Ndwandwe clan, King Zwide, wouldn't allow King Thanjekwayo to partake in the battle, he and King Thanjekwayo came up with a secret plan of only using a couple of warriors from the emaSwati clan during the fight. Those were the warriors who were privileged to know about what King Shaka's warriors' horn-attack did. They had heard it directly from one of Shaka's most trusted warriors, uSoshangane.

Though this information was only known by a select few emaSwati warriors, it worked greatly for the Ndwandwe Kingdom.

When the emaSwati warriors came to the rescue of the Ndwandwe Kingdom, some of the Ndwandwe warriors were badly wounded and already prepared to rather flee for their lives. Then the emaSwati warriors appeared.

To cut a long story short, they were the ones to stop the battle and as few as they were, they forced the Zulu warriors to retreat. They were too well-trained and informed to be beaten by a greater number of warriors. The emaSwati warriors were a shock to both the initial key members at war, the Zulus and the Ndwandwes. When they appeared, the battle stopped for a few seconds as both opponents were still in great shock as to who they were. They went closer and wasted no time in attacking the Zulu warriors like they were nothing.

However, you'd remember that the Zulu warriors' numbers were then tripled by the affiliation of both the Mthethwa and Qwabe warriors whose kingdoms were allied with the Zulu Kingdom at the time.

With or without the assistance of uSoshangane, the emaSwati warriors were still greatly respected by the Zulu Kingdom, along with the Mthethwas and the Qwabes. In simplest of terms, they feared them.

They feared them from the reign of Chief/King Mashobane of the emaSwati Kingdom who led the kingdom through the practices of what he personally presented as *iKhubalo*. This was another form of *muthi*-related practices used to magically harm the enemy. It was said, "*ushaya ngeNduku yekhubalo...*"

Hence, even the name Mashobane was derived from a traditional tool known as *Ishoba* which was widely used by traditional healers. It was made from an animal tail such as a horse. These were used during a process known as *Ukuhlola* or *Ukubhula*, especially in the southern parts of Africa. Isn't this kind of telling us something about "what" rather than "who" the great yet significant figure Mashobane was?

Because he or she who carried *Ishoba* was believed to be able to foresee the future, hence, *Ukuhlola* (to check) which in that context would actually be the future or the past.

Later, this was mistranslated (or rather changed to the present-day Khumalo). When it is mentioned in full, Mashobane becomes a clan name (*izibingo* or *izithakazelo*) representing the presence of the spirit of the significant figure that uMashobane was in their bloodline. This then comes down to the presence of his son's spirit, uMzilikazi.

Hence, this would then be sang or said to be Khumalo-Mzilikazi ka Mashobane.

I guess this answers the connection between uMzilikazi and the Kingdom of emaSwati question. This would also make Shaka and uSoshangane the cousins of who was then King of emaSwati, Thanjekwayo Dlamini. This would also make them close relatives of the emaSwati royal family.

Because, in this portion of our "lost" but significant historical events, we get to be reminded of who these figures were, especially uMzilikazi (the founder of the Ndebele clan) and uSoshangane (the founder of the Tsonga clan). They also had to change their identity as they travelled further afield from the Zulu Kingdom. This was basically history repeating itself, because if you recall, many of these power-hungry figures were actually the descendants of Hebrew ancestry. They knew about kingship from as far as beyond the Exodus when the slaves escaped from Egypt.

This mothered a number of kingdoms thereafter; some towards the north-east of the world which formed Europe. Some went north-westwards and formed America. There was also a spree of empires that were also unnoticed which kept on developing southwards from the North.

This was spreading slowly and was caused by land or territorial and power disputes amongst those who were then "simply leaders", given their abilities being different and admired by the rest. This was until many of their clan slowly developed into kingdoms but which were not entirely led by kings or what people later started knowing as kings or leadership structures.

This means that before our forefathers met with the groups of people who flooded the continent in the name of escaping Egypt, they would only hear about these leadership structures and stories of kings from certain individuals who were said to have been to Egypt. There have always been rumours of what happened in Egypt where some of our forefathers went. Many would leave the rural areas and move to urban areas such as cities in search of greener pastures.

It was believed and famously known that once you go to Egypt, your life would completely change if you returned at all. However, most of this was just rumours about kings and slaves.

This was until the era of the Exodus which resulted in many of those slaves developing the psychology behind king/slave ideology. Later, it was known to be something that belonged to our culture. But, not really…

Okay. Before I lose you, I want us to go back to the year 1818 and the Battle of Mhlathuze.

This will then lead us in the direction of the "wrong" history of the abaNgoni. Many thought that some of it was lost and lost for good, but no!

Not on my watch. Because, just think about what made the kind of information you're reading as we speak about the current history of white men doesn't say about us to be in this very book you're reading now.

Yes, yes, you got it right. It's the spirit of the restless souls of our forefathers who are using me to tell you about what you need to know about yourself, about your origin and what made you the person that you are today.

Okay, let's rewind.

Remember that the Battle of Mhlathuze between the Zulu Kingdom and the Ndwandwe Kingdom was already coming to an end. And yes, the emaSwati warriors, as few as they were, fought against the Zulu Kingdom, which was accompanied by its allies, the Mthethwa and Qwabe kingdoms. And when the Ndwandwe warriors saw emaSwati warriors dominating the battle, they too gained strength and hope. As badly injured as they were, they forgot about this and started to chase the Zulus away. This means that the Zulus did not win the Mhlathuze River Battle, especially if they ran away as that is what ended the battle.

The Zulus were defeated and forced to retreat by the emaSwati clan, despite the initial member of the war being the Ndwandwe clan. So, in short, they won the battle.

And, to add colour to that, you'd recall that a year later, the amaZulu Kingdom went back and picked up the pieces of their fallen dignity and pride during the Battle of Mhlathuze River. They had no choice but to run for their lives from the emaSwati warriors.

1819

Oh! Here's interesting news you'd like to know about both the Ndwandwe and Mthethwa kingdoms. Please learn as it unfolds.

The two notable and significant figures of King Zwide were generals, Ngqaba and Nomahlangene. They were the sons of King Mthethwa, the father of King Dingiswayo and the father-in-law of King Zwide. This then made them either uncles or cousins-in-law of King Zwide who was married into the Mthethwa clan. This made him a son-in-law in the Mthethwa royal family.

So, this then means King Shaka was using Dingiswayo against his so-called sons-in-law's kingdom.

I hope you're hearing why I would say uMzilikazi and uSoshangane shared blood somehow with the Zulu royals as they did with emaSwati Kingdom, especially for them to hold such top positions in the military structure of King Shaka.

So, prior to the battle in 1819 against the Ndwandwe Kingdom, there was a bit of conflict that King Shaka wouldn't have seen coming. But, let's see if he did.

Betrayals And Manipulations

As the generals, Ngqaba and his brother, Nomahlangene were slowly growing concerned about the expansion of Shaka's Kingdom. They made King Zwide understand that (on behalf of their sister who was queen of the Ndwandwe Kingdom). They were not alone in this deadly agenda and worked with the king of the Qwabe clan, Phakathwayo.

And before King Shaka knew it, his allies were now becoming his greatest of enemies. But had King Shaka noticed yet? The answer is not really.

Also, those who worked against a man of Shaka's calibre couldn't do it alone. They also needed some balance in information from people who were very close to the Zulu King. Hence, they even relied on the trusted generals of King Shaka, uMzilikazi and uSoshangane, who were also slightly raising an alarm of turning their backs against him and questioning his leadership.

More than anything else, according to them, King Shaka didn't really realise that he was already creating a situation he was never going to be able to ever contain. He had gone too far and they would hear him say, plan and see him doing things on a regular basis. And remember, if they were older than Shaka, they must have already started families and had wives and kids. They were being deployed from one battle to the next which was planned by the king who was still single and probably mingling at the time.

Somehow, they didn't like what was about to unfairly happen to the abaNgoni clans in general. King Shaka was ready to shake them, if not devour them and turn them into Zulus.

Well, that, without the knowledge of what was had prepared for him. Which if he knew; "people" would die if not "him" before the battle began.

Slowly and silently, uMzilikazi and uSoshangane gained followers from the large bevy of people who were supposed to be the followers of the brutal King Shaka. However, uMzilikazi and uSoshangane's situation was complex because those followers were also divided into two groups. Some leaned their honest trust and hope on Mzilikazi while some leaned theirs on uSoshangane.

They had lived with them for ages. They knew their integrity and goals for the abaNgoni clans. They were honest (okay, though the followers may not have been sure of their honesty) but at least they knew them for almost similar but fair policies. That was also why.

Many of them wouldn't have agreed with King Shaka given the kind of ruler he was. He was arrogant and this later turned into ignorance. Eventually, he lived his life based on negligence. This led to hard times. True hard times.

It is no secret that before the Mthethwas approached Phakathwayo, the king of the Qwabe clan, who was also worried about Shaka's goal to become a powerful king, Shaka had plans to centralise his kingdom by seeking territorial expansion. But, little did he know that that was an era of "every man for himself". Hence, the relationship between uMzilikazi, uSoshangane and the emaSwati Kingdom didn't stop at anything to limit the plans of the Zulu Kingdom's expansion. After all, they all shared the same fear. Great and rapid progress unfolded between these three parties who were then working hand-in-glove with one another.

However, their goals differed based on the growing number of their followers. This was especially the case for uSoshangane and Mzilikazi as opposed to uThanjekwayo who was already a king and to whom the expansion that Shaka was seeking was going to fall into his hands anyway. This meant that Thanjekwayo was the least desperate amongst the three figures. His only concern was the safety of whatever the number of Ngoni Groups that could be possibly saved from Shaka's rule. Starting with the Ndwandwe Kingdom which was already inside Shaka's "oven" waiting to be baked and panned out as Zulus.

This was unlike both uMzilikazi and uSoshangane who possessed an almost similar impact on their group which were already refusing to become part of the Zulu clan. They already possessed their own heritage, pride, dignity, culture and traditions which conflicted with the values of King Shaka.

That's where the wise emaSwati king, Thanjekwayo, came in. He advised uMzilikazi and uSoshangane that it would not be wise to be a single entity and that they should divide themselves into two separate groups to save as many people as possible. Thanjekwayo made them realise that they wouldn't have managed to move quickly when there were too many of them in one group. He also made them realise that by doing so they would gain better positions in the process. He basically made them see themselves as future kings.

King Thanjekwayo was the one behind this plan and he tried his best to make this possible. So, already by this year, uMzilikazi's and uSoshangane's migration plans were already mastered. Basically, they were sorted. Even though based on this plan's timeframe, uMzilikazi first lingered for a bit while uSoshangane had to flee with his followers.

This forced them to help each other rather than work against each other. It was in this very year (1819) that uSoshangane's migration plan was established and unleashed. But wait and hear how this panned out.

Mind you, King Shaka, on the other end, was busy working on his new attack strategy. It was different to the one he used in his first approach to the Ndwandwe Kingdom when his soldiers ended up running for their lives. They ran away from the emaSwati warriors who were too powerful, especially during the reign of uThanjekwayo. Many Ngoni clans saw him as an equal to Shaka in terms of power.

But wait until you hear the entire outcome of the 1819 battle between the Zulus and the Ndwandwe known as the Nyezane Battle. This followed the two battles of the previous year, the Gqoki Hills Battle and the Battle of Ncome which famously became known across Ngoni-speaking clans as *Impi Yase Ncome*.

It is said that this battle turned the Ncome River red with blood. Hence, to this day, it is still called Red River. This battle started over cattle or perhaps what was made to look like cattle conflicts.

The Ndwandwe clan had too much cattle and King Shaka didn't like that. Besides, the Ndwandwe Kingdom was promising to have a brighter future ahead and it was already a huge threat to the Mthethwas and the likes of the Qwabe Kingdom, all of whom were power-hungry and seeking expansion. The leadership of King Shaka was sure making it difficult for them to do so. In short, Shaka wanted it all.

However, the Nyezane Battle between the Ndwandwes and the Zulus became a vehicle for uSoshangane's planned escape. He waited for the day of the battle and prior to that uSoshangane, helped by uMzilikazi, had an operation where they trained uSoshangane's followers. They were a combination of war men and regular nobles of the Kingdom of the Zulus and were taught how to fight and defend themselves. Shaka wouldn't have noticed what was going on as the entire Zulu Kingdom was preparing for the battle.

So, it was hard to identify what uSoshangane and uMzilikazi were sneakily doing against the king in his kingdom. Everything looked normal, like any kingdom would when preparing for war. As king, Shaka enjoyed watching that 'business' and seeing his generals deeply engaged in ensuring the safety of his people (well, of those he thought were his people). He sure must have loved that. And, in his mind, it was just the beginning of a big operation, especially when he saw new faces joining the army. If only he knew.

While this was going on in the Zulu Kingdom, the Ndwandwe Kingdom was also getting ready. Their plan was tricky.

Okay. Perhaps I should begin where it starts. Remember what I said about Zwide's trusted generals who belonged to the Mthethwa clan, Ngqaba and Nomahlangene Mthethwa.

They were gathering information about Shaka's operation from their 'links' who were still within the Mthethwa Kingdom. The information about the battle was easily leaked because at this point in time, the Mthethwas, together with the Qwabes were slowly and silently working against King Shaka. This made it easy for Shaka's plan to be shared amongst his enemies. They found out about Shaka's plan for the upcoming battle, worked against it and it worked.

Three Weeks Before The Nyezane Battle

Zwide's generals led almost half of the army halfway and the ordinary people of the Ndwandwe Kingdom to eSwatini Kingdom. The only ones left behind were half of the Ndwandwe warriors who were prepared for the Zulus. The arrangement involved the emaSwati king, Thanjekwayo, whose kingdom kept on strengthening as it expanded dramatically. uSoshangane and uMzilikazi knew about it all and by the time the Zulu warriors reached the battlefield, they would find a few men and the rest of the men that Shaka's warriors were understandably expecting to fight the battle against. However, they turned out to actually be some members of the troop of Zulu warriors who took their orders from uSoshangane. During the Nyezane Battle, Shaka's warriors ended up fighting with uSoshangane's warriors and followers. Because the battle was fought during the night, it was difficult for Shaka's warriors to even notice that they were fighting with some of their own. As you know, warriors don't ask, they fight whatever stands in their way and that is what the Zulus did.

They were left no choice but to fight as the nature of the battle itself seemed to have been set to be strategic like that. Both the Ndwandwe warriors and those of uSoshangane fought as though they retreated, moving backwards as they fought. However, King Shaka Zulu's troops noticed that Zwide's warriors were somehow but slowly reversing northwards until the radius in which their Ndwandwe Kingdom was passed. It left only a few kilometres' gap between the Ndwandwe Kingdom and what was their destination, eSwatini Kingdom. The intention was to lead the Zulu warriors towards the border of eSwatini where it was planned they would be defeated by the emaSwati warriors who waited restlessly for the battle to come to them. However, Shaka was smart. He saw it coming and suddenly ordered his warriors to stop fighting and retreat.

Here's another thing that you need to know about the Nyezane River. Like many rivers, it was believed to have been possessed by ancient but supernatural creatures known in Ngoni language as *Inyoka Yamanzi* or *Inkanyambha* (mermaid in English). We do not have our name for mermaid in our Ngoni language and these creatures are known as *Inkosazana* or *Indoni-Yamanzi*. Both are completely different species but they both dwell in the water. These creatures were known for their ability to provide some form of phenomenon in the evenings. As a matter of fact, my beautiful grandmother, Agnes Thokozile Malinga (1947), spent most of her childhood in her grandmother's home, Kwa-Gogo Buza, kuGege in eSwatini Kingdom. It is a place which still carries the name of Thanjekwayo as we speak. It is called Kwa-Thanjekwayo.

There was a river crossing a couple of hundred metres away from her grandmother's home but every evening they would experience some kind of bright light. She says that it provided more light than the moon as you'd be able to even pick a needle off the ground. That's how bright it was. It was not the moonlight and it was believed to have been provided by the *Inkanyambha* who regularly appeared when there was no moonlight.

Grandma says that they could even see and witness that the light seemed to have come from the area where the river was. It was in the bottom part of the village in the valley where their river (which was not the Nyezane River) was crossing and heading towards the Kwa-Zulu region.

And, my grandmother says that her grandmother, Khokho Buza (who was born in 1901), would tell them tales of the creature that lived in their river down the road. She told them it used to protect their entire village from any harm. She says that when they asked her more questions about this creature and what it looked like, she would simply reply, "*Yinyoka* (the snake)" or "*Inkanyambha,*" which looked like the head of a horse with scales of a fish and was red in colour. This was someone who grew up in true ancient times (when the so-called gods and goddesses walked the earth). As even my beautiful mother, Ribbon Malinga, the only daughter of Gogo Agnes Thokozile Malinga, who was privileged to be brought up by her mother's grandmother, Khokho Buza, who is said to have shared many stories of these weird creatures that scientists say do not exist. Khokho Buza, who knew this for a fact, was said to have been very lucky when she was a little girl when one day she saw *Inkanyambha* passing by in the sky. It is believed that she said that the creature may have forgotten to hide in the clouds before the rain started because she managed to see its face and its movement. She said that the creature moved its head in a nodding manner (up and down) and looked as though it was struggling to drag its own huge body using its wings. And she said the creature was flying so low that she could even see that it had scales.

It was not only Khokho Buza who knew about these creatures. Some people believed they were seven-headed snake-like creatures who were huge and powerful. It was said that they possessed the ability to provide light, bend air, create strong winds and form rain clouds and make it rain. It was said they would create storms when they were angry and could fly from one place to the next.

However; the point I'm driving home safe here is that this could have been the reason why near the Nyezane or Nyezana River happened to be the best spot for the battle to be fought. Nyezane could have been a word derived from the Ngoni word *Inyezi* (the moon). However, the word possesses a suffix (*isijobelelo*), *-ana* at the end of it. Linguistically, this is to emphasise the grammatical function/properties or aspect of a "word" as per a "unit". Hence, this in our Ngoni language can actually appear at the end as *azi* or *kazi*. In the present-day Zulu language, these are known to be *Isijobelelo Sokunciphisa* (*-ana*) and *Isijobelelo Sokukhulisa* (*- azi*).

For example:

-ana may be used to emphasise a smaller unit of something, e.g. *uMuntu* changes to *uMuntw-ana*, Inyezi changes to Inyez-*ana* (like Nyezana River).

-azi or *kazi* may be used to emphasise the larger unit of something, e.g. *Umfula* changes to *Umfulak-azi* and *Indlu* changes to *Indlu-kazi*.

This then means what they followed towards Nyezana River could have been the light. This may have presented itself exactly like the one my grandmother told me tales about. She also says it looked like *Inyezi* (the moon). This is the ancient word for the moon before the isiZulu language was established and read and written which introduced the word *Inyanga*.

This then retraces me to Shaka's name which could have been referring to a shark. As I'd like to believe that like many other water species, such as fish and the likes, scientifically are said or believed to have fallen from other worlds as a set of bacteria that eventually multiplied into fish. This then means it could have been sharks.

They both live in the sea, right?

And you'd also remember that the scientifically proven study of white revolution says that some people amongst us developed from some fish bacteria from outer Earth.

This was the name that Shaka's mother gave him. However, I'm not too sure whether or not Shaka was referring to what white men's history would say in explaining such a coincidence in names. According to them Shaka means "little beetle" or "intestines". This is said to be a name in the Zulu clan culture but not in abaNgoni clans' culture. There is a difference because not every Ngoni is a Zulu or belongs to the "Zulu family". So, Shaka was a name that white people knew about. However, the biggest problem here was the isiZulu Language which came with great manipulation of words. Many were mistranslated and transformed from their original Ngoni language meanings into present-day isiZulu language which was in honour of King Shaka Zulu.

During the year when the isiZulu language was established, it was the year when many words had already been transformed and it happened before it was officially announced as isiZulu language. It was actually the year when a lot about our heritage and culture faded as our ancient language was destroyed to form one that the amaZulu clan were only able to influence when it was formed.

For example:

Thabatha (old abaNgoni language)................

Thatha (isiZulu language)

Hence, the word to refer to *isibhaklabhakla* (something which is too huge to explain) was shortened to sound as *isibhakabhaka* (sky). Our forefathers called it *IsiBhaklabhakla*, referring to the wideness and gigantic fabric that our blue atmosphere was and still is.

And then here's another phrase to which the greatness of *uMvelingqangi* (aboNgoni god of understanding) was also influenced to sound like.

This was simply because no white man at the time could pronounce the word *uMvelingqangi* so they stacked it with our forefathers' statement of emphasis to which his presence was magnified and amplified through. They would normally say, "*uMvelingqangi... oMkhulu kaKhulu*" (*uMvelingqangi* who's greater than great). That was transformed into a mess of a word which sounds like *Nkulunkulu* which sounds whitish.

But, I still bet that white people still struggle to pronounce it or any of the abovementioned words to this date. This very initiative and generosity to change our God's name to what suited their slow learning disability was mainly done to help accommodate their "failure" to speak our language like we speak theirs.

Our heritage was compromised so that they could easily pronounce the isiZulu language and engage with our culture much more easily; the very same culture that was later stolen. Lol!

So, I think you can see where I come from to be "fooled" by the white man's history about myself. How does that even work?

For an enemy to write a proper history about the stories of their own enemies and their culture of destroying ours.

That's why it doesn't make sense at some point because European writers were only after cash. And they saw a gap in our forefathers not being able to write and read and document their own stories. The rich history that Africa contains was exactly what they were after, and of course, to steal the abaNgoni culture and methods of living.

That's why you won't know the meaning of your "being" because it was fabricated by white people. Then they left and became millionaires in their countries using your stories.

That's why even the name of Shaka Zulu would be changed for meanings that hid their "dirty hands' engagement" in the capturing of kingdoms. And, no one questioned it because everyone seemed to have grown a habit or a weird behaviour of all of a sudden trusting white people to could preserve the best of history (in their own books).

Forgive me but I think it's naive to trust that their yesterday's enemy could preserve the best of history for them tomorrow. How does that even work?

Please find me. I'm lost.

I'm not sure if you understand this but it is all true but hard to believe and understand. I sure believe that it understandably sounds like a lie when what you've been consuming the most in your previous life was "the lies".

Look, Shaka's name before he became Shaka Zulu was known to be Senzangakhona ka Mthethwa. He inherited the name of his father, Senzangakhona ka Jama. However, his surname proved to have been from another clan than that of Jama to which his successor became Senzangakhona Ka-Jama Dlamini.

This then gives us another angle as to what may have made King Shaka grow up with Mthethwa clan in the first place because he never belonged to the Dlamini clan. He grew up a sick child who was a weak boy while he was with the Dlaminis. Hence, his truer clan name (*izibingo* or *izithakazelo*) was actually that of the Mthethwa clan, biologically so. That became a Dlamini by right as Shaka's mother, Nandi ka Langeni, insisted that uSenzangakhona was the father of Shaka.

That's because Nandi's pregnancy was reported to the Dlaminis by the ema-Langeni clan who descended from the emaSwati Kingdom which was Jama's Kingdom and the one Shaka changed into the Zulu Kingdom.

But Shaka's life was one which was a bit tricky to understand. He had a connection with some creatures known as *Izilo-Zengubo* who directly gave orders to *Abalozi* (ancient beings who communicated in a

whistling language. They'd actually whistle to speak).
Izilo-zengubo were humanoids and lived in both the
waters and on land. However, they were only on land
for short-term operations. They possessed powerful
magical abilities as they belonged to the generation of
the creatures from the moon *(Phe-Zulu)*. Among them
were the biblical fallen angels, so-called Nepheline,
known to have invaded Planet Earth millions of Earth
years ago.

The *Izilo-Zengubo* had dark-greyish-skins. Some
would appear greenish. Their bodies were layered
with wet, hanging cloth-like fabrics and fibres of what
looked like a violently wriggled blazer or long jacket.
These would often be covered in mud for protection
against the sun. However, you would barely see them
on land. If it happened that you did, you were considered very fortunate indeed.

But, once you got to witness one of these creatures
with your naked eye, it was known by the elderly that
you were the "chosen one" and indeed, after a few
days, if not a few weeks later, you'd disappear. You
would then return powerful and wealthy.

They worked with a group of ancient beings called
Abalozi. They were known for their magical abilities such as becoming invisible. It was the connection
that Shaka had with those creatures which made him
powerful. I can't say they made him king because the
Mthethwa and Qwabe clans played a great part in
ensuring that Shaka became king. It may have also

been the plan of Shaka's secret gods but I cannot confirm that.

Izilo-Zengubo were very powerful creatures who could retrace past events and foresee what was about to happen in the near or far future.

Hence, they were a part of the cluster of creatures which were worshipped as *Amadlozi* (ancestry) as opposed to aba*Thonga* (spirits of the dead). The other group, *Abalozi,* preferred travelling at night. This group comprised powerful pathfinders whom only King Shaka could see.

Abalozi were a group of men and women who sacrificed themselves to the Abaloyi community, who would normally sacrifice their integrity, language and culture and adhere to that of *Abaloyi*. This is a Ngoni word or name derived from *uku-Laya* (to cause harm on purpose). It would then sound as *Abalayi* but later, when the isiZulu language was first documented, it was such suspicious, obvious and direct words and names that were the first to be changed.

This then makes me understand why Shaka's names were changed into completely different meanings from the direct meanings they each possessed.

This could have been the direct meanings that both of his names possessed which made their meanings to be too obvious and too direct and therefore changed.

This is especially true if you're buying the narrative of the revolution that gave birth to man from fish.

Which then says in volume as to why Shaka claimed that he belonged to *Emkhathini* (space). Hence, his surname Zulu which was a short way of saying *phe-Zulu* (heavens to Christians and *Phe-Zulu* or beyond the sky or *Emkhathini* to cultured people).

To this day, it is believed that the community of *Abaloyi* (witches) would normally meet at *Emkhathini* (space) at midnight. This is when they would be deployed to carry out their duties according to their individual positions and ranks.

And then, as we may have discussed this narrative of fish, it therefore means that sharks belong to outer Earth. This could be where Shaka, from time to time, would claim that he belonged. Because yes, the name Shaka may have been a gift from his mother, the princess who never was, Nandi ka Langeni. She may have known something about her son and hence, she named him Shaka.

This does invite a number of questions. For starters, how would the abaNgoni people, who till this day spend 99.9% of their lives on land, get to know about sharks? This is especially true of the generation of that era who wouldn't have known about sharks. Even if they did, why does this name sound like many which are known as *Amagama Mbholeko* (borrowed words from other languages such as English and Afrikaans)? In our geographical history's context, these would be words or names that abaNgoni's grammar and vocabulary or our forefathers didn't have in their languages.

This means these were a cluster of words and names that were brought to existence by the existence of white people in our lives. They came with the ships.

However, despite his name being uShaka and having no attachments to sharks, he also seemed obsessed with seeing blood just like a shark.

Oops! Okay!

Back to the Nyezane River scenario which to me becomes a link as to why most of Shaka's battles were fought near rivers. Despite the knowledge that I have that many of those rivers worked as borders separating the existing kingdoms, there may be another reason for this.

This is especially because of the connection Shaka had with the creatures of the waters, *Izilo-Zengubo*. This pushed him to want to have most of his battles near rivers rather than on plain ground. Okay, I guess we should go back to the battlefield.

We were on the part where the Ndwandwe warriors and the followers of uSoshangane were heading northwards to eSwatini Kingdom.

This made the Zulu Kingdom the victors of that empty battle.

Why do I say it was empty? Because it was planned to pan out as it did. You will recall that Shaka was a proud man and that from time to time he would say he was connected to the waters and was never easy to defeat near water. uSoshangane and Mzilikazi knew that like the back of their hands that Shaka's power was in the waters.

So, that was the game plan they used to defeat him. The emaSwati warriors were ordered to rather not engage until the battle reached the Swati border post. This was another way of distancing the Zulu warriors from the actual Nyazana River.

Besides, like I mentioned about the Nyezana name's origin and what I mentioned about *Inkanyambha's* way of providing "the light". So, the further the distance the Ndwandwe warriors and the followers of uSoshangane created from the actual river, the better. It became darker and this then forced the Zulu warriors to retreat by default. But, remember that King Shaka was also wise in his own way. He knew that something was not right about that battle. He put all the blame on uSoshangane given what was already planned to be the connection to uSoshangane's random escape. This also left most of Shaka's warriors and King Dingiswayo and uSoshangane's men lying dead on the ground. And unfortunately on uSoshangane's side, there were also a lot of dead bodies amongst the few but badly wounded men that he had left as an army.

But, before I move forward, I want to share with you the intelligence that uSoshangane used on that evening. Remember, he was still King Shaka's general. He led the battle but was invisible to Shaka. Remember, that to beat a wolf, you have to be a wolf yourself. This means that even though King Shaka was able to know about the future, he wouldn't have when uSoshangane was protected by *muthi* from being easily seen by Shaka. Sure, Shaka may have known that something would go wrong but he couldn't figure out what it was. Hence, as the Nyezane Battle continued he was able to know that something was not right.

He did well by calling for a "seize fire" before the battle reached the emaSwati borders. This was where the emaSwati warriors would only look as though they fought in defence of their kingdom rather than fighting as allies of the Ndwandwe clan. That was King Thanjekwayo's plan. He was the mastermind behind it all.

However, Shaka's seize-fire call worked for him and his warriors. When they returned, they realised that amongst the murdered men scattered on the ground along the Nyezane River was the body of his mentor and father-figure, King Dingiswayo. He was probably murdered by the followers of uSoshangane before they broke apart from what was meant to be the troop of King Shaka Zulu.

You will recall that three weeks prior to the battle, King Zwide's generals, uNgqaba ka Mthethwa and his brother, Nomahlangene, had migrated at least half of the kingdom, including warriors of the Ndwandwe clan, to the emaSwati Kingdom. However, Mdlalose ka Mthethwa, who was also Zwide's general from the Mthethwa clan, remained with the rest of the warriors who awaited the Zulu warriors. Most of all, it was to help identify his cousin-brother, King Dingiswayo amongst the Zulu warriors.

It was their conflict with Dingiswayo which caused them to break away and join the clan to which their sister was married, the Ndwandwes. Dingiswayo had chosen Shaka over them and mentored him to become king when they thought Shaka never belonged to the Mthethwa Kingdom. The conflict leading to their breaking away made them hate Dingiswayo who, according to the three of them (Ngqaba, Nomahlangene and Mdlalose ka Mthethwa), both King Shaka and Dingiswayo were supposed to die.

They knew very well about both Shaka's and Dingiswayo's plans. They knew this from when they stayed in the Mthethwa Kingdom before they left and they knew what damage it would cause. This may also have been another reason why Dingiswayo and Shaka were so obsessed with destroying the Ndwandwe Kingdom. However, Zwide's generals planned well. They made it look like a defeat when it was in fact a trap. Zwide's generals also had their own target. This meant that even if the Zulu warriors continued chasing them, they'd be chasing their own death.

Wisely, the king of the Zulus ordered his warriors to rather return and have a slight check at the kingdom of the Ndwandwe clan. He didn't understand what was happening and thought it would be wise to head directly to the Ndwandwe Kingdom for answers. And of course, have a look, you know.

However, they found nothing. Not even smoke or dogs barking. The cattle and other valuables were nowhere to be found. Basically, the kingdom was literally empty!

You should have seen the anger and the frustration that King Shaka had after realising that he had been played for a fool.

And I'd be angry if I were him too. The dude was played!

At least King Zwide never left him with nothing to express his anger on. There were still a few buildings standing in the Ndwandwe Kingdom which King Shaka burnt to the ground in anger and frustration.

So, yes. That's how he became the victor of what I still call an empty Battle of eNyezana River.

The Zulu/Mthethwa Clash

As you'd recall that prior to the Nyezana Battle, there were already some manipulative stunts that were orchestrated secretly by the Mthethwa and Qwabe kingdoms. This was a movement against King Shaka; and was driven by fear of being added to the statistics of the fallen kingdoms. The expansion of the Zulu Kingdom created great concerns for both King Phakathwayo and King Dingiswayo's successor, Jobe ka Khayi.

Besides, King Shaka was no longer himself after uSoshangane had escaped. He trusted no one including both kingdoms. He thought they had something to do with uSoshangane's escape and the death of King Dingiswayo who was his father figure and mentor. This caused serious tension between them.

However, it started with the Mthethwa clan after Dingiswayo had passed on and Jobe was then king of the Mthethwa Kingdom. Jobe ka Khayi never liked Shaka very much. He saw him as a great threat to his kingdom.

Jobe had a series of arguments followed by Shaka's lack of trust in almost everyone. He was beginning to annoy the Mthethwa king, Jobe Ka Khayi, who later expressed his opinion on how Shaka was treating his own people. This may have forced uShoshangane to flee. Remember, King Jobe did not fear Shaka.

Hence, their argument never took much time to ignite into serious conflicts, one of which ended up jeopardising the close relationship between them (the Zulus and the Mthethwas). But before we move any further, Shaka's real surname was Mthethwa. I hope you still remember that.

This also added to the pile of conflicts which led to the famous clash between these two great kingdoms.

Look, in the first place, the Mthethwas kingdom expansion campaign was was more powerful than Shaka thought he was himself. King Dingiswayo had full knowledge of this, especially being the one to play a huge role in making him become king. The deal was to strategise to make Shaka the king of the Dlaminis (because Senzangakhona's surname was Dlamini). He wanted to capture the Senzangakhona Kingdom while in the process enhancing his chances of his own kingdom expanding.

But, even if King Jobe knew about that operation, he wouldn't have done much about it. He and King Shaka were already not on good terms for him to have used the channels of Dingiswayo.

Fast Forward

This was all done secretly by white people. Everything that abaNgoni suffered was conducted by white people. The Shakas and the likes were all the products of white men who were already in the shadows.

The eSwatini Kingdom remains and the Zulu Kingdom changed into KwaZulu-Natal Province. This speaks volumes.

Look, the aim of this was never really about Shaka's history but that of Thanjekwayo.

cozi-cozi yaphela.

The Last Word

Look, I may not be an expert in tracing blood-lines but trust me, I know that abaNgoni people belong together as one group on Planet Earth. I know that we were all developed from one surname (Nguni) and that the oldest of all surnames is Mnguni.

Many abaNgoni clans developed from that. If there's any surname that can be older than this one, it must have been those which were "documented" by white people to be "old".

The newer races (Indians, Chinese and later whites) are a generation of Adam. As such, according to them, the oldest surname can only be Adam, who both he and Eve were scientifically and magically made in the Garden of Eden rather than created. That's why it is said they were created in God's image. On the other hand, your forefathers, as the abaNgoni race, were the first to be created for and with the life of Earth and against the life of Earth. This makes them the oldest and the first to have ever existed. It is a white lie that they were once baboons and slowly changed to being men and women (our present-day parents). If you believe in that white nonsense, you must have been brainwashed too.

And I want to share you a story, a story that I still think and believe was shared with me by something very powerful. It is a story about "us" and "them" or what separates us from them, apart from the fact that they were made and we were created.

Our forefathers were never baboons. However, in the early stages of life they spoke or communicated in "brain language", without any verbalised words or voices. They used sounds to express their emotions etc. Since the beginning of life on Earth, our forefathers have always known who they were. They knew that their purposes weren't in alignment with any evil or misconduct. Hence, even during the Stone Age when the present-day time was meaningless, they still called and knew themselves as abaNgoni people (those who never sin). It is true they knew nothing about sins therefore, they never sinned.

This was until white people were made while their Gods were witnessed falling down from the heavens. That's exactly the narrative I'd like us to discuss. That's because there's actually no such thing as Heaven as much as there's nothing like hell. That is nonsense.

Look, I don't care whether you think I'm racist or not. That's where whites and them would jump to when facts are being told about them and their differences rather than similarities with us. And that's simple to understand, especially to me (I'm not speaking for nobody here but myself). We're not the same people as much as our purposes will never be the same either.

Some speak and some don't. That's what makes us not the same as abaNgoni people (the rightful origins of planet Earth).

And from where I'm standing, those who speak have become less in number. That's because the "system" deals with them for exposing the kinds of unrealistic realities that people have been made to believe and convinced of being "life" and therefore "reality" when none of it actually is.

It is sad that many wake up in the morning ready to live "real lives" but the reality of this age is that there is nothing "real" until people remember who they truly are. Do you remember the question I asked earlier?

How do you feel about the life that you're calling "real" when it is not? How do you feel?

I'd already be feeling stupid by now if some white dude who came from nowhere told (and I believe him) that my forefathers were demons.

Lol! Excuse me. Not for me, please!

That's madness. So, how do you feel when you look down on yourself so you look good to someone else? Doesn't that feel like you're being controlled by something you don't even know? It is powerful to set your mind free to see that you're "captured".

Because that's what has happened to many people. They have been captured. They cannot see reality and see themselves for who they truly are. I mentioned the device being used on you for you to be an enemy of yourself. It's called Masonic Mind Control.

It dates back to the ancient times of the Samaritans or the Annunaki group. They were aliens from Planet Niburu whose intention was to fight against everything that was happening in Egypt. Hence, today you know Egypt (Africa) as a bad place. That's why many Africans to this date can't wait to see themselves in Europe and the likes because they're so convinced that that's where life is.

Lol!

That's rubbish!

What are Europeans doing all over Africa if in Europe there's "that" kind of life?

Look, never be fooled by a white man here. White people cannot and hear me out right, CANNOT, do without us. We're the button pressers of Earth's life. It is our breathing that is keeping them alive. I'm not talking about whites, Indians and Chinese here. No, I'm not. I'm talking about the abaNgoni people, the owners of Planet Earth. Hear me out. Nothing will ever go right in any of the three abovementioned groups without us. For we're the heart of this planet, not them.

Lol! Just when I was beginning to live with these creatures, 2020 came and I was like, "Okay, tools down."

I am not fixing any relationship of mine with any of these creatures. I learnt from them that you can even call a person an animal. That's why I feel free to call them what I (not other African people) feel like calling them. They can call us animals and that is why I don't give a f*ck how a white man feels when he is called an animal. In fact, it feels great.

And, this is not revenge but me saying what I like about white people and they can't do anything about that. Because not even killing me will make a white person's life better. They've wronged us greatly to feel any better about anything. They don't feel anymore, do they?

Unlike many books, I'm sure this will be a completely different book. Because it says exactly how a white person came into the picture. Yes, it is true that white people are alien offspring and they are abundant here to carry out duties.

And their duty, like it has been of their god/aliens is to collect data and to destroy the true life of Earth, fulfilling the wishes and desires of their angry gods.

That's why they've been digging our planet. Yes, abaNgoni's planet for millions of years and taking our mineral deposits. Some think that eventually Earth will die just as many other planets did. This includes many of their own origin, leading to uncountable alien groups lingering in the sky in flying saucers, UFOs or "ships" as their offspring call them.

It is never a coincidence that a white person hates you and will forever hate and look down on you. No! It is never a coincidence that they were carefully made to be like that by the enemies of our own forefathers. Their gods/aliens if you like. If you meet a white person who says that they love African people, he or she is broke.

Because all those who are rich just wish (though it will never happen) that you weren't here and that they remained. Just like Bill Gates and his devil-worshipping friends, if they're not the devil themselves.

Who is this other South African one again?

Nicky Open-what...Oh! Heimer. I know what these guys are about and the agenda they had of depopulation in Africa because they claim that we're worthless and contributing nothing to the global economy and therefore, we deserve to die. That is why I started hating on them proudly. Oh! And that spooky, ugly daughter of Bill Gates that appeared in their evil videos about Africans not deserving to live. I just don't like them and for simply that. Who are they? Gods?

And, that's when you see that white people don't think (well not all of them because some are adopting to be man these days) but the rest are just a bunch of rubbish. You know why. They also think we're a bunch of rubbish, that's why!

And, me not being a Christian and against all the crazy system of white men allows me to speak of how I feel and the way I like. Just like a white person.

I won't forgive a white person in my life for they'll never stop hating me either. So, as they continue, I'll do likewise. Like, who cares?

And you know why I speak the way I speak. I don't fear death and I don't have fear. No! And death is for us all. I am mentioning this because the kind of thinkers of my fashion are a huge threat to the system or to white people and their gods (aliens).

And if you are black and you're reading this book now, please be assured of the intentions of this book. This is not for you to believe what I believe. This is not a book for you to follow in my footsteps and it is not a book for fun. Instead, it tells about the kind of truth that white people want or thought was "classified". Classified! My finger!

The truth that touches white people is known to be Illegal and harmful.

Illegal and harmful? My ass.

They should have thought of that when they started looking down on us. They acted as if they wanted nothing from us but they wanted all that our fore-fathers had, including the culture and traditions. They killed our people and tried to force them into religion. They sold our brothers and sisters as slaves in Europe just like they are used to selling what they produce. They should have thought of what was illegal and harmful.

Now, there's no time to bow to minors. White people are minors. In this life on Earth (which is ours) they weigh nothing! I just wish every African, whether or not they are Ngonis, will know this from me if they haven't been hearing it elsewhere.

White people are the ones worthless in this life. And the greatest fear that they have is of you. That's because they think we'll never know about them and where they came from.

Nah!

We've always been one step ahead of whites and them, especially in terms of understanding where they came from. Many white people are hearing it from Africans that they don't belong here and that their forefathers lied to them. But, not ours who shared great stories of who they were.

Hence, it is our secret that the truer meaning to understand who white people are can only be understood by abaNgoni people. It was them who came up with the white man's name, *beluNgu.* This gives it proper meaning only when you read it backwards. Hence, you can see that I had to position the capital letter "N" in the beginning point of the word or name for these creatures. Lol! But, please do me a favour and read this backwards.

Our forefathers were wise people. Hopefully, you'll understand that I possess love but only for my people, my forefathers whom I love greatly for the wisdom they carried in them,

It goes without saying that they were always a few steps ahead of them in terms of wisdom. While they were part-time calling us animals, we call them pigs on a daily basis.

Because *Belungu* when read backwards says *Ngulube* (pig).

And to all who were brainwashed, this will land rough as it's not even expected to land on white people themselves. That's because there is a group of "whitish-african people", like your current president, Cyril Ramaphosa. He is a great example of a white person's puppet. He and the likes of I'm not sure whether I should call Honourable Mandela and Mugabe or what. They just make me sick!

But at least not too sick to not say what I like — like a white person about a black person and no cares; right?

But, trust me, I know that the group of brainwashed Africans will be the ones ranting and chanting on behalf of whites. You know what white people would rather do? Hire a black dude to kill someone like me who is making abaNgoni understand that white people are basically nothing.

Lol!

I laughed the other day when I was watching a TV show about IQ levels between a one-day-old baby of an African and that of a white man. A white baby's brain at the age of one day does not function. It is like there's nothing there. On the other hand, the African child's brain is already active and doing stuff. So, these people are nothing without aliens, of course.

Because even the technology they're boasting about and are very greedy with doesn't even belong to them but aliens. They make deals with aliens in exchange for what looks like wealth, power and fame. And, there's actually nothing there. If you remove the media, the cameras and news writers, you'll see that there's actually nothing that white people have that is considered "organic". Their nature is to be against nature. Like, who the hell in seven earths needs a god of violence?

But, you'll find one when follow deeper into the god of Christianity where you get to hear about the god of earthquakes, the god of war etc., everything which sounds scary and evil.

They came with the Bible that says, "Thou shall not kill," but they've been killing us for hundreds of years.

"Thou shall not steal" but they're the ones busy stealing from us.

"Thou shall..." Thou, my foot!

African people need to wake up now. Especially the group who call themselves Christians. Even then, I'm not talking about the Christians who are enjoying being evil and toxic to their own families. I am talking about those who need light.

Because some do know that Christianity is an evil cult and their God is Satan. Some do know that and they don't have any issue with it. They love Satan. He's been there for them, helping them hate and divide.

Look, until Africans are feeling free to stand up and talk about what they feel about white people even if it's hurt — like white people are doing it to them even if it hurts.

Umhlaba wobaba mkhulu bethu; uyobuyela ezandleni zendlu emdaka.

We need to speak out! That's what we need because we can't keep on making everything about white shenanigans a secret! Nah!

That's why this book is not like other books whose writers are only after money and fame; not their own content, not their own emotions. Because these are those writers who are writing to sound nice to white people because when you don't, your book, like many of mine, stands a chance of not being published. Yes, that's what happens when you speak facts about the system.

But will that stop me from doing it? Nah! I'm not writing for either money or fame but for the dignity and the pride of our forefathers who are as we speak restlessly seeing the change in what they left behind as sons and daughters.

So, the time to speak out is actually not tomorrow but today. Speak out!

And say what you feel. It's okay.

THE END